The Drugs Menace

The Drugs Menace

MARY MANNING

Foreword by
Michael Meacher, MP

COLUMBUS BOOKS
LONDON

Copyright © 1985 Mary Manning

First published in Great Britain by
Columbus Books
Devonshire House, 29 Elmfield Road,
Bromley, Kent BR1 1LT

British Library Cataloguing in Publication Data

Manning, Mary, 1925–
    The drugs menace.
    1. Youth——Great Britain——Drug use
    I. Title
    362.2'93'088054   HV5824.Y68
    ISBN 0-86287-179-4

Designed by Liz Hubbard
Typeset by Inforum Ltd, Portsmouth
Printed and bound by Clark Constable,
Edinburgh, London, Melbourne

The author of the poem that opens Chapter 2 is Detective
Constable Brendan Farrell of Merseyside Drugs Squad. It has been
set to music by Paul Shooter and made into a record sponsored by
The Wirral Globe. Any profits from sales of this record will go to the
newspaper's Drug Abuse Fund, which has been set up to help local
voluntary groups. Enquiries to: Martin Hovden, Managing
Editor, *The Wirral Globe*, 29 Seaview Road, Wallasey, Merseyside,
tel. 051 630 6030.

Contents

Acknowledgements

I wish to thank everyone who has helped with interviews and information during the preparation of this book, and to say how much I appreciate their generosity in giving of their time and knowledge. I am especially indebted to the staff of SCODA, the Standing Conference of Drug Abuse, in London and Glasgow, for the information which they provided in relation to services throughout Britain. I am grateful to the BBC for permission to quote from the BBC1 documentary film *The Pushers*, and the Radio 4 *Checkpoint* programme on anabolic steroids.

A special word of thanks is due to Joan Keogh and her colleagues at PADA in the Wirral, to the many members of Families Anonymous, and to those with drug problems, for their kindness in sharing their personal experiences with me and with readers. (Fictitious names have been given to all those cited who are currently coping with drug problems.)

Finally, I wish to express my appreciation for the help obtained from the studies of the numerous researchers and authors who are quoted in this book.

MARY MANNING

Foreword

In the past year drug abuse has received extensive publicity. While public awareness has been heightened, resulting in increased pressure for a positive government response, both action and resources have fallen short of dealing with this complex and widespread problem. Home Office figures confirm that drug abuse is no longer limited to a small minority, as was the case in the 1960s. It is growing at a rapid pace, is endemic in all social classes and all age groups and, most alarmingly, it has become rampant among schoolchildren.

Britain is in the throes of a drug explosion, and it leaves those who argue that drug abuse is related to psychological illness – a manifestation of personal deficiencies – at a loss to justify their case. The explosion cannot be ascribed to any mass change in personality, but what we *can* point to are profound changes in people's environments. Economic growth has been replaced by decline and stagnation, unemployment has risen sharply, especially among women, young people, unskilled workers and minority groups. Many live in inner-city areas where housing is deteriorating, transport and other services are being cut and large areas of industrial land lie barren and vandalized. It is hard for anyone not to experience a growing sense of cynicism and despair in such circumstances, particularly young people faced with a less than 30 per cent chance of getting a job – a vacuum which extends indefinitely into the future.

While it is obviously not the case that all heroin-users are going to be poor or unemployed, any more than full-time work in the home drives people to tranquillizers and sedatives, a sense of personal futility inevitably contributes towards a tendency to drug abuse. A recent Home Office report accepts this relationship, pointing out that 'social and economic deprivations are likely to aggravate some of the deleterious effects of drug abuse'. While making frequent reference to the need for a general crackdown on drug availability, the government has so far been totally silent over the report's recommendations for alleviating drug abuse in terms of policies 'directed towards the well-being of society, including measures for redistributing wealth and reducing unemployment'.

It has a vested interest in doing so. Changing the day-to-day reality of most people's lives – the stress of a consumer-oriented society, the endless parade of unattainable lifestyles in the media, the drudgery and boredom of unskilled work, and the disintegration of family bonds, which leaves women and the young unemployed in particular isolated in the hostile environment of multi-storey estates – would mean changing the basis of our society, which rewards the few at the expense of the many. In the early days of capitalism religion was 'the opium of the people'. One-hundred-and-fifty years later opium itself, along with other drugs, has become 'the heart of a heartless world'.

Controlling the supplies of drugs both legal and illegal is vital if we are to limit the increase in the numbers of drug abusers. But this is only of indirect benefit to individuals and their families. A cutback in supplies for those already physically and psychologically dependent has major implications for health service provision. As far as illegal drugs are concerned there is the additional danger that crime rates may increase even further to finance scarce supplies.

Effective treatment and rehabilitation services for drug-users – whether young people experimenting or chronic drug-users – need to focus on a multiple approach that includes facilities for drug counselling, medical treatment, detoxification and if necessary rehabilitation in a drug-free community.

As far as provision in the statutory sector is concerned the picture is very gloomy, reflecting the lack of government commitment. Between the 15 English regional health authorities there are fewer than 200 beds for special use by drug abusers. The few drug clinics in existence are almost exclusively based in big cities, particularly London. It is fair to say that we haven't even a skeleton service for coping with drug abuse, yet central government continues to stress that it is for each region to decide for itself the level and type of resources needed.

However, local health authorities are no longer able to make the provisions needed by their local communities: the money simply isn't there, because the government has relentlessly cut the NHS budget. Faced with the prospect of having to select which existing services are going to survive, it seems naïve if not openly dishonest for the government to assume that drug-treatment facilities will spring up as and when decided by the different regions. Neither does the government's attitude go any way towards meeting the point that there are known to be authorities which are not sympathetic to the need to provide services for drug-users. As with alcohol, the traditional attitude that it is up to individuals to 'pull themselves together' still lingers, both within and outside the health service.

Moreover, funding from local level takes no account of changing patterns in drug use. The problem is by no means confined to major conurbations: while it may be less obvious in rural areas, drug abuse in isolated communities is as prevalent as anywhere else. If funding is left wholly to each local area those with a small drug-taking population will inevitably be hard-pressed to devote money to projects not widely used by local communities. The provision of specialist units providing facilities for patients from a wide area would circumvent this difficulty. Overall planning and funding would also help ensure that unnecessary duplication does not occur.

The role of the voluntary sector is also important. Not only are non-statutory agencies already providing services which reflect long-standing experience in the field; many drug-users, particularly young people, are reluctant initially to approach official services, finding them less sympathetic than voluntary agencies. Yet little progress can be made in the treatment and rehabilitation of drug-users without the provision of a comprehensive service – and one which is not unduly bureaucratic.

Coming to terms with drug abuse does not, however, mean a ragbag of policies mixed with precarious short-term funding such as is currently being offered by central government.

What is needed is a national policy to combat drug abuse; a co-ordinated national strategy involving statutory and non-statutory sectors with access to adequate levels of finance. Such a national policy might include, for example, such proposals as a review of GPs' prescribing practices; a ban on prescriptions of opiates or synthetic opiates by the private sector; withdrawal of product licences for drugs which have been superseded by more effective or safer products and a thorough review of customs regulations and procedures.

To date £12 million has been made available by the government on a 'pump-priming' basis. Two million pounds has been allocated to the launch in spring 1985 of an 'educational and information campaign' aimed at alerting parents and their children to the dangers of heroin addiction.

At the time of writing £10 million has been made available to the health regions as part of a national campaign against drug abuse: a sum that is grossly inadequate. (The Standing Conference on Drug Abuse estimates a minimum requirement of £20 million on present-day costs.)

Health authorities were invited to submit their schemes to the government for funding decisions, but as this was done on an entirely *ad hoc* basis there has been no overall assessment of the problem or identification of priorities. Those schemes to which funds have been awarded have usually been given sums so far below the amount of money needed that schemes can be neither of the quality nor of the nature intended.

Moreover, the nationwide survey of drug abuse by the health authorities due for completion in December 1984 has still not been submitted. Despite this, the government has started allocating money, without knowing where the need is greatest.

In *The Drugs Menace* Mary Manning emphasizes the tragedy which confronts an ever-increasing number of parents when they discover their child is abusing drugs. She points out what they can do as individuals and where they can go for help. Unfortunately, the difficulties which many of these parents have encountered in their desperate search for help and support only highlight the urgency for a realistic government policy towards the cancer of drug abuse.

MICHAEL MEACHER, MP
March 1985

1 'Most of my friends are dead . . .'

In his vision of the future machinations of Big Brother, something which George Orwell, the author of *1984*, failed to predict was that the real 1984 would be the year when heroin addiction featured almost daily in every national newspaper and no parent or child could ignore its ever-present threat.

It was the year when rock star Pete Townshend shook the nation with an impassioned appeal at the Conservative Party's annual conference. 'I was a heroin addict,' he admitted. 'I survived, but most of my friends are dead.'

He mentioned legendary names of the rock world: Keith Moon, drummer with The Who; Jimi Hendrix; Brian Jones; Janis Joplin. All were cut down in their prime by the drugs menace after tragically short careers.

Also at the conference was the Oxford sixth-former Colin Dobson, who told the gathering that drug-taking was widespread among 12-year-olds in his own comprehensive school. This confirmed reports that had been circulating for some years about schoolchildren in London, Edinburgh, Glasgow, Liverpool and Dublin – and a growing number of other towns throughout Britain – for whom heroin had become a daily necessity.

This was the year in which Australian Prime Minister Bob Hawke broke down and wept before a television audience during a discussion on drug-trafficking. The cause of his anguish, it was later revealed, was the heroin addiction of his own youngest daughter and her husband. In Britain, there was public dismay when the wife of a popular actor described their 22-year-old son's habit as 'just a bit of fun'. A thoughtless remark, perhaps, aimed at an intrusive microphone . . . but alarming in terms of its potential to spread such notions of 'fun'.

This was also the year when, in the United States, David Kennedy, son of the late Senator Robert Kennedy, was found dead in a lonely Palm Beach hotel room after swallowing a lethal drugs 'cocktail'. For him the road to addiction and death had begun with an experimental smoke – of heroin – during a visit to New York at the age of fifteen.

It was the year when many young lives were lost in Britain, too. For some, the end followed a gradual downward spiral. For others, it was sudden and unexpected, as in the case of young Lady Gormanston, who choked to death after inhaling a mixture of heroin and cocaine at a party. It was sudden, also, for rock drummer Wells Kelly, who collapsed and died after sniffing a similar 'speedball' mix of heroin and cocaine.

Yet there are youngsters – and older people who should presumably know better – who say that heroin is not really a dangerous drug if taken in 'reasonable' amounts. How little they know, and how tragic that ignorance is.

Not so long ago, heroin abuse was looked upon as a highly expensive and decidedly depraved pursuit, compared, for example, with smoking cannabis. Even seasoned drug experimenters tended to give it a wide berth. One reformed drug-addict, Alan, who experimented with just about anything that came his way during the early 'seventies, recalls that he always drew the line there. 'Never with smack – never with heroin,' he insists: 'Even if you could afford it, you had to be really far gone to shoot up that stuff.'

Why, suddenly, was heroin part of the national consciousness? Following political changes in producing countries during 1980 and 1981, there was an influx of heroin that was infinitely cheaper than had formerly been the case. Its low price, and the fact that it could be sniffed or smoked, rather than injected, made it seem almost harmless to the uninitiated.

'At the peak of public anxiety about drug abuse in the late 'sixties and early 'seventies there were something like 2,000 heroin addicts in Britain. Now we are thinking in terms of about 50,000. We are talking about massively increased amounts of street heroin now available at a much cheaper price, which makes it financially possible for many more young people to try the drug,' explains Dr John Strang, regional

2

specialist in drug dependence at Prestwich Hospital in Manchester. The fact that treatment services have not expanded to cope with the growing problem should be, he claims, a cause of national concern.

Official estimates of the current extent of heroin abuse in Britain are believed to represent only a fraction of the true total. The latest Home Office figures in respect of *new* notifications of heroin addicts show a steady increase from 1,110 in 1979 to 2,117 in 1982 and 3,559 in 1983. While these figures are seen as a useful indicator, it is recognized that they represent only a small proportion of those with serious problems who seek treatment under the National Health Service. And even those with a will to try to beat the habit are often discouraged by the lack of treatment facilities.

Describing himself as 'the father of a heroin addict who has experienced, like many others, the appalling deficiencies in the present system of drug abuse treatment', a Swindon surgeon wrote: 'Facilities for the treatment of drug misusers are nonexistent in many areas of the United Kingdom. Few doctors either in hospital or in general practice want to treat drug-abusers, nor do they have the knowledge and training necessary' (*British Medical Journal*, 26 January 1985).

Only one in five heavy users of heroin and other opiate drugs is receiving treatment now, compared with one in two twelve years ago, according to researchers of the Drug Indicators Project at University College Hospital, London, which has been studying the problem since 1980. Delays of six weeks to six months for a first appointment at a hospital clinic are fairly standard, and all too often the young person's resolution to overcome the drug habit has gone off the boil by the time the call comes; otherwise, he may be in prison for possession of drugs or for theft – embarked upon to support the habit.

Doctors expressed their concern about this situation at a two-day conference of local medical committees of the British Medical Association in June 1984. A proposal put forward by London GP Dr Eleanor Butler called for a substantial increase in clinics and support groups to help meet the needs of younger drug-users and their families. Doctors from Scotland, Birmingham and Manchester spoke of the urgent need for local initiatives to be taken. Drug addiction, one speaker claims, should be treated as a 'highly infective and dangerous illness' (*British Medical Journal*, 7 July 1984).

The growing problem in Merseyside was discussed by a Liverpool GP, who revealed that the city of Liverpool did not have a single drug dependence clinic. The nearest clinic was at Chester, a distance of 25–30 miles away, where the waiting time for appointments was over twelve weeks. On the other hand it was pointed out that a patient with a sexually transmitted disease could be treated immediately at a walk-in clinic in the city.

However, the consensus of opinion was that drug abuse was not purely a doctors' problem. It was also a social problem calling for social support and financing, both locally and through central government.

In the whole of Britain there were fewer than 300 specialist hospital beds for people with drug problems and a mere 100 other beds in ordinary hospitals, in the spring of 1984. Most of these facilities were in the south of England. Moreover it is claimed that the National Health Service has out-patient facilities for only 2,000 addicts – again, mostly in the south-east. There is no evidence that any substantial improvements have been made in response to recent pressures.

As Dr Angela Burr, lecturer at the Addiction Research Unit at the Institute of Psychiatry, London, observed in her review of the Granada Television documentary series *Heroin* (*British Medical Journal*, 12 November 1983), such figures 'highlight the woeful inadequacy of drug treatment services' in Britain.

The television series focused attention on the recent spread of heroin abuse in Edinburgh, where an estimated one in twelve of younger people were said to be affected in certain areas. Among those specifically mentioned were Pilton and Muirhouse, two large, decaying housing estates with high unemployment and few facilities. Yet the one Edinburgh hospital with provision for addicts had only four beds for them, and only one of these was allocated to Pilton and Muirhouse.

Between 1977 and 1983 the annual total of drug addicts notified to the Home Office roughly trebled, rising from 3,600 to over 10,000, and since 1980 notifications of new addicts have been rising at an average rate of nearly 40 per cent per year, according to a report from the Drug Indicators Project by Dr Richard Hartnoll, its senior research psychologist: 'Since 1977 nearly all of this rise has been due to heroin as the principal drug of addiction, with only a slight increase in other opiates such as methadone and Diconal. Whereas in 1956, 56 per cent of first notifications involved heroin as the principal drug of addiction, the figure was 85 per cent in 1983.'

According to a report in *The Times* (8 October 1984) the British share of the thriving heroin black market is reported to be worth £200 million annually, with a street value of £80,000 a kilogram. Another cause for concern is that on the street heroin is not only cheaper but purer than ever before. This was stressed by Dr Tom Waller, medical adviser to City Roads Crisis Intervention, in a *General Practitioner* report (18 May 1984).

The purity of street heroin in Britain varies from 5 per cent to 90 per cent, with an average purity level of 46 per cent. By contrast, illicit heroin seized in the United States has an average purity of only 5 per cent. Taking these facts together, Dr Waller argued that even if 90 per cent of all illicit heroin were seized, there would still be enough in circulation to provide all current users with heroin of a standard comparable with that found in the United States. Or, looked at in another way, there is enough illicit heroin now coming into Britain to supply about 300,000 regular users.

It is estimated that about 10–20 per cent of illicit drugs are being seized by police and customs officers. At a time when there has been a four-fold increase in heroin smuggling, there has been an 11 per cent reduction in customs staff (with a loss of 1,000 jobs), according to the officers' union, the Society of Civil and Public Servants. Travellers entering the country at present have a less than one per cent risk of being stopped for inspection; and 90 per cent of freight coming through British ports is no longer subject to customs control. It is even suggested that recent spectacular successes (more than £100 million worth of smuggled drugs seized in 1984) might be seen as a measure of larger and more frequent smuggling operations.

While there has been a good deal of publicity about increasing heroin abuse among working-class adolescents in urban

5

areas, there is evidence to indicate much more widespread abuse among young people in all social groups, though not in black or other minority communities. According to Dr Hartnoll's report, the majority of heroin-users are aged between 15 and 45, with a peak incidence among 20–29-year-olds. There are two male users for every female user at present.

In addition to their shared dependence on drugs, one problem which young users in all social groups have in common is an inability to find treatment promptly when they need it. Now that professional people are 'going public' to protest at the dearth of provision for treatment they discover when their own children need help, it is manifestly clear that the development of services has been a hit-and-miss process.

According to Dr Tom Waller there are no facilities at all in many parts of Britain. Even in London there are two boroughs which are not served by a drug dependence unit. He warns that the future looks far from bright with regard to new projects being set up with money from the government's current 'pump-priming' scheme. Once the three-year funding commitment comes to an end, there is no guarantee that fresh funding will be forthcoming from scarce local authority resources. (We have seen this happen before in the case of valuable social initiatives launched with high hopes in the 1960s and 1970s.)

Dr Waller calls attention to the precarious position of the street agencies and non-statutory rehabilitation centres, which have held the fort for so long in this field. Funding bodies on which they depended have either gone already or are on their way out (the London Boroughs Association and the Greater London Council are two of these), and charitable trusts report an ever-increasing demand for help from their usually limited resources.

What this critical shortage of provision means in practice is that there is seldom anywhere to which someone using drugs can be admitted at short notice, except in an emergency involving immediate risk to life. Therefore it is not surprising that for many parents, arrest and a spell in detention are seen as the only chance of finding a drug-free environment and some form of rehabilitation for their child. While, as some authorities suggest, a short, sharp shock of this kind may do a lot to bring some

6

youngsters to their senses, treating problem drug-users in this way makes even less sense than locking up chronic alcoholics did in the past. Moreover, it is a very costly way of dealing with the problem.

'The cost of keeping drug-users in prison, estimated to be in the region of £200 a week, has to be balanced against what it would cost to put the same drug-user into some kind of re-habilitation and residential centre. The Standing Conference on Drug Abuse costs the latter at around £100 a week – a 50 per cent saving on simply locking up drug addicts,' explained Michael Meacher MP in his 1985 report, *Cold Comfort.* 'Added to this consideration is the likely effect on users' habits when in prison. As a recent report by the Prison Officers Association shows, there is no shortage of drugs in our prisons.'

Britain is not alone in having a serious drug problem which has grown up virtually overnight in many areas. During 1984, illicit traffic in heroin reached an unprecedented level in most parts of the world, according to a report in January 1985 by the International Narcotics Control Board (INCB), a United Na-tions body based in Vienna. In the European region alone, 1,500 people died in 1983 as a result of drug abuse. In many areas, drug trafficking and drug abuse had become so pervasive that entire economies and legal institutions were being dis-rupted.

The INCB report provides a realistic yardstick against which to assess the arguments of those who still insist that it is the parents' fault if their children take to drugs or some other form of anti-social behaviour. Clearly, the deciding factor in the current spread of heroin misuse in areas like Glasgow, Man-chester, Merseyside, the West Midlands, and the Irish capital – Dublin – has been easy availability and relative cheapness.

'A sudden surge in "addictive personalities" is an unlikely explanation for rapid changes in the overall pattern of heroin use and availability,' says Dr Richard Hartnoll, referring to another familiar argument: the role of personality and family background as possible precipitators in various forms of addic-tion. This argument has been explored at great length by many authoritative observers. One point of view is that it is funda-mental to the 'blame the victim' syndrome, which suggests that the problem rests with the victim and he must change himself, rather than the fault lying within the community and being due largely to social problems. However, the factors seen as paramount in the current spread of heroin abuse are availability of the drug and the involvement of close friends and classmates. As Dr Burr sees it, 'The spread of heroin use among unemployed and deprived youngsters . . . is clearly a response to the lack of employment opportunities and the frustration and poverty of these youngsters' everyday lives.'

So is drug abuse a medical or a social problem? Are problem drug-takers ill or deviant? 'This uncertainty is at the root of a lot of the difficulties we encounter in trying to help addicts,' asserts Dr Strang, the Manchester specialist. 'But . . . no single description can be used satisfactorily to fit every drug-taker. There are personality and environmental influences at work in each case, and one person's use of heroin may be a greater source of concern than that of another person.'

While the current increase in heroin abuse is depressing news, there are, on the other hand, some encouraging signs. Dr Strang explains: 'The characteristics of those involved seem to be changing, and don't fit into the typical medical model of a "junkie". In the north-west we are beginning to see people with much more varied patterns of drug abuse: short-term users and people in stable marriages, who are pleased to have people who will help them to come off drugs.

'There is no universal answer which will help everyone with a drug problem, so we must tailor our response to the individual's particular needs. Some people can be treated as out-patients; some may need residential care in a hospital unit or sheltered hostel; so we need a range of services. We should also be concerned to help those who do not wish to make a change in their drug-using behaviour, so that they run less risk of becoming a casualty. We should be trying to set up user-friendly drop-in services to make it easier for drug-users to enter into treatment.'

Dr Strang stresses the importance of statutory services in the treatment of heroin abuse. Parents' groups and other volunteer support groups have a valuable role to play, but their involvement must not be seen by the authorities as a substitute for the professional services needed. One cause for which voluntary pressure groups could campaign is the right of drug-users to general medical services. 'There is no justification for doctors in casualty departments to discriminate against drug-users and refuse to treat them,' he observes.

It is not only hospital medical staff who are reluctant to treat drug-users. Many family doctors take the same attitude, and complaints that addicts are unable to get on to GPs' lists are commonplace. Yet because of the limitations of their lifestyle (which may be typified by poor nutrition, chronic chest infection and insomnia), drug-users often have a much greater need than others for regular medical check-ups and treatment. Where the drug-user is adolescent, such situations become doubly critical.

It is precisely because drug-users need more medical attention that some doctors do not want them as patients, as one young GP explained at a recent conference on heroin addiction. Another wrote in *Medical News:* 'I don't have the time or the will to help addicts. Addicts are very manipulative people. They are abusive to receptionists, they create mayhem in the waiting-room . . .'

Another correspondent, a London doctor, was more tolerant: 'If someone wanted to give up and had nowhere else to go, I would consider it my duty to help in any way I could.'

Though there have been successful partnerships between GPs concerned to help drug addicts and some voluntary agencies – such as the Blenheim Project in West London – the overall picture is still one of woefully inadequate treatment facilities. Clearly, it is the hope of the government that many more GPs will in future take a closer interest in the problem of heroin addiction and drug problems in general. Indeed, this hope was spelt out in the Minister of Health's new guidelines on the treatment of all forms of drug addiction, sent to family doctors throughout Britain in October 1984. In this document doctors were reminded that the Department of Health and Social Security has a duty to treat people with drug problems and that doctors should consider all of the individual's needs as well as the specific drug-related problem. But the Minister admits that drug addicts 'are not always the most popular and responsible of patients'.

Yet serious physical complaints requiring medical attention are all too common among 'hard' drug-users, as was shown in a revealing study by an Edinburgh GP, Dr J. R. Robertson (*British Medical Journal*, 5 January 1985). About half of a study group of 46 people who had injected heroin at some time were found to have had illnesses directly related to their drug use: 38 per cent had suffered from jaundice; 5 per cent from bacterial endocarditis (infection of the heart's lining and valves); and there were many cases of abscesses and infected veins; 62 per cent admitted to sharing hypodermic needles with other drug-users.

Drugs other than heroin used by members of the group at some time included cannabis (38 per cent); DF118, a synthetic opiate (36 per cent); Valium (31 per cent); Diconal (30 per cent); barbiturates (22 per cent); cocaine (22 per cent); amphetamines (12 per cent); methadone (8 per cent); morphine (8 per cent); LSD (6 per cent).

There were 28 men and 18 women in the study, with an average age of 22½ years. The average age at which they had begun using heroin was 18¾ years. Most had been introduced to the drug by a friend, and all had bought drugs in the vicinity of Dr Robertson's practice, which is situated in an area of council housing estates. The most encouraging finding of the study was the high proportion of those involved who had managed to give up using opiates for long periods without supportive treatment of any kind. Fourteen people reported periods of abstinence lasting for 6 months, and 11 reported abstinences of 1–6 months.

In 1985 the government is funding over 80 projects for a three-year period from a total of £12 million being spent on preventive measures and treatment programmes in the fight against drug abuse. Some of this work is described in Chapter 5, on treatment strategies. Though a great deal more money is needed, there are signs that local authorities plan to fund initiatives to help meet demand in their own areas.

Two parliamentary enquiries focusing on heroin abuse were launched early in 1985. One, chaired by Mrs Renee Short MP, is seeking evidence from doctors and professional organizations in order to be able to recommend the best ways of treating and rehabilitating those who misuse hard drugs. A parallel home affairs committee enquiry is seeking to establish the true extent of drug abuse in Britain. Meanwhile, publicity measures designed to counteract the growing trend towards increased misuse of heroin amongst youngsters include a government-sponsored television campaign and education programme. Aimed at parents and school-age audiences, these depict the grim consequences of drug abuse.

Prevention is always preferable to cure, of course, and in the case of heroin abuse there are many stages at which intervention can be useful. But the most effective step possible which could be taken would be to cut off supplies before they enter the United Kingdom.

Seizures of smuggled heroin during 1984 included one 36-pound haul said to have a saleable value of £2,500,000. It was the largest seizure ever made at a ferry port, yet it represented only a small percentage of the heroin which could be intercepted if the number of customs officers were to be restored to the level existing before cuts were imposed by the government on the grounds of economy.

Government action must of course be paramount in the campaign against the drugs menace. But it is also a matter requiring the urgent attention of every parent, for no young child or adolescent can be regarded as immune from this threat. The issue calls for constant vigilance within families, and campaigning energy for action at local as well as national level.

What steps can ordinary individuals take to protect the nation's youth? The first is to arm ourselves with knowledge about heroin and other drugs, and to be aware of signs which may indicate a risk-laden pastime or friendship – or the sheer boredom of an aimless existence, which has led all too many youngsters to experiment.

2   *Not in our family*

What on earth have I done to my life,
  Oh where will it all end?
All for a little package of dust
  That I used to call my friend.
They told me that it was no harm,
Just smoke it and you'll feel good,
So I chased my little dragon friend
  As hard as ever I could.
But oh, the misery it has caused
  To me and to everyone,
All my belongings have now been sold,
  And I'm living in this slum.
What on earth have I done to my life,
  Oh where will it all end?
All for a little packet of dust
  That I used to call my friend.
I had three friends last year,
  Now I'm down to one
They all started 'cranking up',
  Each and everyone.

You see, after a time you need so much
  Of that little packet of dust,
So you put it in a 'set of works',
  To satisfy your lust.
But in the end it gets you.
  That little dragon – yes.
I know I'm going to join my friends,
  To that I must confess.
Oh what on earth have I done to my life,
  Oh where will it all end?
All for that little packet of dust
  That I know is not my friend.
The pains are coming back to me,
  I need a bag right away,
Where on earth will I find one?
  I've not got the money to pay.
Perhaps I'll get a 'lay-on'
  Off Alan, George or Jed.
No way – there is no chance of that,
  For they are all now dead.

'The Dragon Who Used To Be My Friend', Brendon Farrell

* Chasing the dragon: smoking heroin
* Cranking up: injecting

* Set of works: hypodermic syringe
* Lay-on: supply on credit

It was late evening. John, aged fifteen, had not yet returned from a visit to a friend, a call on a drug-pusher, and a spot of theft – of something many times the value of the £5 bag of heroin he would receive in exchange for it.

'Never leave your handbag unattended with an addict in the house,' his mother had warned me earlier. 'The one thought always uppermost in his mind is where to find money for his next fix.'

John does not like talking about the stealing he finds necessary to pay for his drugs. He feels ashamed and apprehensive.

While his mother no longer presses him for details of such activities, she worries constantly when he is out of the house after school hours.

'I dread every knock on the door,' she confided, 'thinking it may be a policeman to say he is in hospital as a result of an overdose – or that he was caught and beaten up while breaking into someone's house.'

Eventually John arrived home, visibly shivering in his thin clothes; inwardly, however, he was at peace with himself for the time being. As he stretched out in front of the fire to absorb the heat, he felt relaxed enough to talk about the habit itself, and its financial demands.

You could just manage on £10 a day, he said, if you were very sparing in your use of heroin. But you couldn't get much of a kick from one smoke; you need several to feel really relaxed and keep the withdrawal pains at bay. Most kids he knew spent considerably more each day, and he himself had used up to £70 worth of heroin in one day on occasion.

'You don't think about saving some for tomorrow,' he explained. 'You just keep on smoking while it lasts.'

When I first met John, a week earlier, I had been immediately impressed by his natural friendliness and the warmth of his shy smile. But I had also been struck by the tragic waste of youthful energy in the grip of a lethal compulsion, which had left him virtually an invalid at an age when his more fortunate contemporaries were preoccupied with sports, girlfriends and school examinations. After talking to me for a while he had become restless and had gone to his bedroom for another smoke. When he emerged, incoherent and seemingly 'high' on the drug, he was soon complaining of stomach pains. Soon he could be heard in the bathroom – groaning, retching and vomiting. 'This often happens if they misjudge the dose,' said his mother.

'If youngsters could only see this side of it before they begin. But John had no idea what he was getting into when he took some heroin for a dare one day after school. He was well hooked by the time we found out about it, and now the habit has taken over his whole life. He has a permanent cold in the head, he has no appetite, he can't sleep, he gets no enjoyment out of anything except the drug. He hasn't eaten a proper meal for four days, and he hasn't got a stitch of warm clothing because he sells everything we buy him to get drugs.'

John and his parents live in a London suburb, but their experiences are no different from those of many other parents up and down Britain and further afield: heroin addiction is an international epidemic.

'We used to think that heroin addicts were people you only read about in the newspapers – pop stars and poor little rich kids,' John's father said. 'At first I thought it was a question of finding the right kind of specialist who would cure him, and it was a great shock to find that there is so little help for young-sters like him.'

No one understands better the initial shock, the overwhelm-ing sense of despair and the social isolation involved in discover-ing one's child is addicted than Joan Keogh, two of whose three sons became heroin addicts.

Joan Keogh is founder and chairman of Parents Against Drug Abuse (PADA), the self-help support group based in the Wirral peninsula, near Liverpool, formed when she discovered how little help was on offer for addicted youngsters throughout the area.

'I found out about the youngest when he was fifteen and still at school. There was a telephone call from the school saying, "I think your boy is on drugs, Mrs Keogh."

'I was sure that my son was going to die. So I rushed about hysterically trying to find help. The first person I spoke to was the family doctor, but he couldn't do anything except put my son's name down for the local hospital, where there was a six-month waiting list. I telephoned the hospital myself, but they couldn't give any immediate help unless he had taken an overdose and could be admitted as an emergency case. Then I went to the school and said I didn't know where to turn. The Deputy Head spent ages on the telephone trying to find some-one who could do something, but it was hopeless . . .'

The school holidays were just starting, and Mrs Keogh decided that the only thing she could do was to keep her youngest son indoors the whole time so that he would not have access to drugs. He did not seem to mind the restriction and he did not appear to have any problems which could be described as withdrawal symptoms, so she began to think he was not really addicted. Besides, she had an additional worry – she had discovered that her second son, then aged seventeen, was addicted to heroin. He was attending the local hospital.

'At the time I wondered how this could have happened to my sons without my being aware that something was wrong, and it was only through searching my memory that I could recognize the tell-tale signs that should have warned me – if I had known enough about the dangers. There were symptoms like rashes round the mouth and perpetual colds, which were worrying – but I never suspected that they were due to glue-sniffing, which they were. There was a time when one of them had a troublesome cough and a poor appetite for ages. I was very worried, but never once thought that drugs could be to blame.'

Joan Keogh soon found she was not the only parent in the Wirral with this predicament, although many, like her previously, might not yet have become aware of their children's addiction. Learning about her sons' drug problems had been a shattering experience for Mrs Keogh, but it had provided her with an unlooked-for insight into the heroin sub-culture which had grown up surreptitiously among the children of the Wirral. Before long she discovered the identities of many other children in her neighbourhood who were also addicted.

'It's very difficult to have to approach other parents – maybe people you don't even know – and have to break the news to them that a child is on drugs. Yet once you know about it, you feel you have to do something,' says Joan Keogh. 'In the end, no matter how tactful you try to be, you find yourself blurting it out: "Your child is on drugs – and so is mine." But it usually turned out that they were relieved to be able to talk to someone about their children, because they were already worried about their behaviour.'

While most of the parents approached in this way had no suspicion that their children were taking drugs, they soon found that they and Mrs Keogh had a torment in common: their children were stealing from them.

'Parents feel terribly ashamed about this – they feel they are to blame for their children being delinquent and couldn't bear to talk to anyone about it in the ordinary way,' continued Mrs Keogh. 'At least that is something they can get into perspective once they realize that stealing is part of the drug abuse pattern.'

One of the more obvious social symptoms of a high rate of drugs abuse in any area is a dramatic rise in the rate of juvenile crime, arising out of the need to support an expensive habit. A frustrating aspect of the Wirral campaign in its early days was the insistence of police and local officials that the existing high crime rate was not drug-related. Within a year, however, police had revised their views about the extent of the problem in the area and were working more closely with parents in efforts to deal with it.

'The first thing we did as a group was to organize a meeting which we publicized through notices in shops and local radio announcements. The fact that we were concerned with drug abuse attracted the attention of the media. When I rang the local radio station to ask them to mention our meeting, I found myself being interviewed on the 10 am news. Over 100 people attended our first meeting, and we found that we were able to put pressure on the authorities to get something done, even if progress has been slow so far. We also discovered that children as young as ten years of age were on drugs, and that babies were being born as drug addicts at our local hospital.'

We all have our own ideas about what the actual mechanics of drug-taking involve, usually derived from films, television documentaries and newspaper accounts – if we are lucky enough never to have encountered the real thing. We know about reefer smoking and 'mainlining' injected drugs, and, more recently, the craze for 'snorting' cocaine in some circles. So what precisely does this new procedure, 'smoking' heroin, mean? Since the operation is normally confined to the privacy of the young addict's bedroom, if he uses the drug at home, few parents have the chance to observe it – and most would rather not suffer the added pain of such a nerve-wracking experience.

One parent who felt she had to know what smoking heroin involved was Mike's mother, an active campaigner against drug abuse. 'I stopped him one day as he came home and was about to go upstairs. I said, "If you're going to smoke this stuff I want to know how you do it. If I'm going to campaign against drugs I want to know what I'm talking about.' So he sat down, reluctantly, and went through his usual routine.

'He had this tiny bag which seemed empty to start with, and he emptied out a small amount of powder on to the kitchen table. He used a razor blade to cut the powder into portions – a minute scrap here, another there. When he seemed satisfied with his measurements I noticed what looked like a few specks of powder on one side and I said, "You're forgetting those few specks," and he said, "No, I'm keeping that for tomorrow."

'Then, very carefully, he moved one of the small portions on to a piece of tinfoil. He used a match to heat the underside of the foil so that the powder gave off fumes. He used a small rolled-up paper tube to suck the fumes up into his throat. Then he held the smoke in his lungs for as long as he could before breathing out again.

' "Is that all there is to it?" I asked, and he said, "Yes." By this time I could feel my nerves going to pieces, and I wanted to rush out and tell everyone, "This is what it's like – this is what our children are being turned into criminals for." The reality seemed so meaningless!'

The 'traditional' method of sucking up heroin fumes is through a rolled £5 note, but any other piece of paper of suitable size and thickness will do, as Mike, aged seventeen, explained later. 'Some people sniff it through the nose but that doesn't give much of a lift. Anyway, you wouldn't get any good out of one smoke – you need a bag at least to make you feel relaxed.'

'It relaxes you – that is all the youngsters seem to be able to say about it if you ask them,' Joan Keogh commented. 'I was talking to an addict one day when I visited a crisis centre in London, and I asked him if the effect felt like being drunk, so that you lost your inhibitions and forgot your cares. "It's more than that," he said. "The only way I could explain it is to say that it's better than sex, and getting off heroin is like the end of a great love-affair. Just imagine sitting at home feeling miserable and desolated over the loss of a girlfriend or boyfriend. You don't want to live any longer, and yet you know that if that person walked through the door, everything would be rosy again. That is how it feels when you decide to go for another fix to the nearest pusher." I've told that story to some addicts and

17

they only laughed, saying that they weren't interested in sex anyway – and that's another aspect of drug abuse.'

In any case, few younger users have the maturity or experience to enable them to discuss their addiction in such lyrical terms.

'We see a lot more of the agony than the ecstasy,' Mike's mother said. 'The best I could say for the drug is that it brought him comfort when he was in great pain through withdrawal symptoms. Drug-taking is a very lonely experience, and Mike knows this only too well when withdrawal pains begin and he says, "I'm getting strung out" . . . he has no one to turn to except his parents – and the pusher.'

Mike's health had improved a great deal during a spell in youth custody some months earlier. He had gained weight, was sleeping well and seemed to have forgotten about drugs for the time being. But he was soon hooked on them as badly as ever once he was free, despite promises to keep off them, and his health had deteriorated again.

'There is no such thing as a regular medical check-up for these youngsters, and our own doctor certainly takes no interest,' said his mother. 'I think a lot of GPs are nervous about getting involved with kids on drugs – they don't trust them to co-operate in any form of treatment.'

The outlook for young heroin addicts is bleak, unless the right kind of help is available, and unless the young person's will to beat the habit is strong enough to win through in the face of constant temptation and frequent setbacks. All parents have tales to tell of recovery which proved short-lived, and the impossibility of the offspring kicking the habit permanently while mixing with friends who are still on drugs.

Needless to say, the effects on the families of young addicts are often devastating. As one father describes it, 'There is no aspect of family life which isn't affected. It strikes you in the home – in the relationship between parents, between them and the addict, and involving other children in the family, until everyone feels that the only solution is to split apart and escape from this nightmare. But it affects the family's relationship with neighbours and with the whole community too. One day you're going about your business under the impression that you have a certain standing among your neighbours; the next thing you know is that your child has probably stolen from them and will do so again. This situation is very hard to live with, but it is nothing compared to the tragedy being acted out inside your home.'

Apart from the initial shock and the heartbreak of seeing a beloved child's health being put at risk by an enemy over which they have no control, parents have to live through the painful trauma of trying to 'come to terms' with a growing loss of hope and of their future expectations for their child.

'We had visions of him following our footsteps into teaching, but even if he could begin to want to pull himself together now there is so much catching up needed that I can't see it happening,' a London mother said.

In Liverpool, a devoted father commented, in reference to the plight of his three teenage addict sons: 'I lived my life on the understanding that from the day I left school I would work and be responsible for myself, and for my family when I had one. They have never taken responsibility for anything, and they are not fit to take responsibility.'

'A plague that creeps in overnight' was how the insidious spread of heroin abuse in Merseyside was described by the father of an addict at one public meeting: 'One morning I happened to look up and noticed that the TV aerial was missing from the roof of my house. It had been taken down during the night by my son and his friend. That is the sort of reality that ordinary parents in ordinary, well-adjusted homes are having to cope with on a daily basis. But the most crucial reality is the fact that if you were to visit our community it would take you less than ten minutes to find a 24-hour heroin supply service where all you have to do is push a fiver through the door and get a little bag of heroin in exchange.'

Youngsters caught up in today's heroin epidemic come from every kind of social background – usually from home environments so 'normal' that parents are very slow to suspect addiction.

'I always thought that "hard" drug abuse was something poor little rich kids got into. I didn't know there was a drug problem in our neighbourhood until a colleague said she thought my daughter was experimenting. I didn't believe a word of it at first, but she was right,' a London teacher told me.

Factors such as the relative cheapness of heroin in the 'eighties and its widespread distribution have combined to make it accessible to younger children from working-class families. The way into addiction for most youngsters tends to be through the offer of a free smoke from a friend or even a pusher. But in the experience of Joan Keogh and her colleagues, progression to heroin from earlier solvent abuse and experimentation with 'soft' drugs is only too common. Before the present crisis arose, young middle-class addicts tended to be somewhat older – late teens, early twenties – when they became addicted, often during visits to cities such as Amsterdam where drug-trafficking is rife; but this pattern is changing.

A woman doctor whose family life was being wrecked by the behaviour of an addicted daughter described the strain of carrying on a daily job of high responsibility while struggling with chaos at home.

'At work people see me as a competent doctor who can be relied upon to behave responsibly at all times and maintain a good relationship with other staff and patients. But beneath all this I'm the demented parent of a 16-year-old girl whose lifestyle is tearing our home apart. I really wish I could run away.'

At a parents' support meeting, other parents in the same position described their experiences: one addict's mother had had her vacuum cleaner taken that day; a father who was already over £200 in debt told the group, 'My gas and electricity meters have been broken into three times this year . . . and there is no one I suspect more than my own son'; another parent was unashamed to admit, 'Today he [an addicted son] was sent to prison for 128 days, so we're hoping for a bit of peace until after Christmas.'

A mother whose son had been in Risley Remand Centre for 26 weeks spoke of the 'wonderful peace' the family had enjoyed in his absence: they knew where he was, that he was out of reach of hard drugs, living a disciplined life with adequate sleep and a reasonable diet, and not stealing.

While one member of the group spoke of an American

psychiatrist who advocated a tougher approach ('You have to stop thinking of your son as the lovely little boy he was and start thinking of him as a thief and drug addict'), many said the police were their only hope in trying to straighten out a young addict's life, and the police were not always helpful.

One addict's mother recalled her experiences, which follow the usual pattern. 'The addict starts sneaking out things you seldom use, and when these have gone they go on to more obvious household equipment. Once you find out you can never trust that child again.' When the family's television set disappeared, she went to the police in the hope that it might be recovered and her son's activities would be brought under control.

She was horrified when the police officer chided her: 'You seem to be trying to make a criminal of your son for the sake of a few hundred pounds' worth of property. I think you should go home and tell him that you're sorry.'

On the other hand, there is no doubt that for the police coping with parents who accuse their own children of theft is no easy task, especially if, as happened in the Wirral area at first, officials deny the existence of any drug problem.

The saddest story of this particular evening was told by parents who had already lost one son, aged eighteen, through drug abuse three years earlier, and were now suffering torture because his younger brother was also addicted to heroin. They had never before talked openly about their troubles to other parents.

'He has never come to terms with his brother's death,' said the mother, speaking of her younger son, 'despite two courses of psychiatric treatment. He has tried to kill himself several times – once by jumping into the Mersey at high tide. He has been in hospital for three weeks but wouldn't co-operate. He has spent two months in prison for handling stolen property. He goes round the house begging 'Will you lend us a fiver?' until I feel like screaming, but I give in very often in the hope of keeping him away from crime. Our family is split and devastated by all of this, but I couldn't live with myself if I were to throw him out, which is what some professionals advise.'

'Tough love' describes an approach to treatment advocated

21

by an American self-help organization of the same name. Parents are advised to tell their child that he can remain at home only if he agrees to give up drugs and start treatment. Some-times, if the threat of being turned out seems serious enough, the teenager makes an effort to co-operate. Some British pa-rents say it has worked well with older sons and daughters who found it impossible to fend for themselves away from home. But specialists warn that this is a 'make or break' approach with obvious dangers for immature boys and girls.

Immaturity is a characteristic of people who turn to drugs, according to Joan Keogh, who recalled a recent conversation she had had with a recovering addict. Now 24, he had been taking drugs since the age of fifteen and was in his fifth month of treatment.

'Because he was used to being preoccupied with drugs during all of his waking hours for nine years he didn't know what to do with his time when he stopped the habit. When he was advised to take up previous interests again, he found that he had to go back to the age of fifteen again because he had done nothing in those nine years. He said he found himself growing younger in a sense, and having to begin to grow up all over again. Isn't that a terrible waste? For years their lives revolve around the drug, and when they try to stop they are bored and depressed – as if they were in a vacuum because there is nothing to rush out for any more.'

Although most of those attending the meeting of Wirral parents were unable to report much progress – and some said they had cast their teenagers adrift, temporarily at least ('when something snapped and I reached breaking point') – a few were hopeful because their children had started having treatment.

One youngster who had been addicted since the age of sixteen seemed to be benefiting from two spells as a patient at a Manchester hospital which provides good supportive treatment after discharge.

'He often telephones the hospital if he gets worried and agitated,' explained his mother, 'and a member of staff there is available to him 24 hours a day. If his own key-worker isn't available, arrangements will be made for another worker to call him back and talk to him for as long as it takes to "bring him down", so that he ends up very calm. He is being very co-operative because he knows this is the last chance he will ever get from me. It's so hard to see a young chap being in and out of prison for six years and returning to drugs as soon as he is free.'

The great moral support to be gained from participation in a self-help group was strongly evident during this meeting. In the course of the evening discussion became more general and long-standing members were able to help put the fears and anxieties of newcomers into perspective.

'I feel so bad and so guilty because sometimes I think I hate this changeling – this twitching, frail creature who follows me about playing on my sympathy. Now, when I've nothing left in the house, I've at last found the courage to tell him I won't try to do any more unless he starts treatment. I've learnt to be calm and to switch myself off, so that I don't respond or react, and that certainly is good for me,' said one of the mothers present.

A community worker stressed the importance of parents maintaining their own emotional strength, and mustering their emotional resources for the time in the future when the young-ster expresses the wish to give up drugs: then, he will need every ounce of support you can give him. Backing this view, a father warned: 'You have to get back to being in charge of your own life, because while you are floundering around feeling hopeless and desperate he is in charge of your life, and that's no good for either of you.'

'Of course, you feel a lot of hate in your heart, but he will understand if you say, "I love you but I hate what you're doing",' a mother added.

But starting to make the break from addiction can be a protracted strain on both the suffering youngster and the parent standing by with support and comfort. A Scottish mother explained: 'They know from experience that it's going to be very hard doing "cold turkey" and getting off drugs without professional help, because they go through similar symptoms to a small extent every time they feel the need for a fix. The trouble is that once they've got themselves to the point of wanting to stop it's very hard for them to stay off drugs on their own, especially when they are in contact with friends who are still using them.'

Timing can be a crucial factor in the decision to go 'cold turkey', since this is a process which will affect the life of the whole family for at least several days. When Ian decided he wanted to stop taking drugs one weekend, he chose the very day when guests were expected for a family wedding. There was nothing for it but to ask him to postpone the attempt.

'It was such bad luck, as we had waited a long time for him to get to this point,' recalled his mother. 'But it really was out of the question that weekend. He would have been sprawled all day on the settee, wracked with pain in his back and stomach and probably vomiting. He would be shivering and going from hot to cold from one minute to the next. Gradually, the pains would get worse until he was a mass of pain from head to toe, and he wouldn't sleep at all for perhaps 48 hours or longer. Even when the symptoms improved he would still not be able to sleep except dozing for short periods. During all of this he needs someone there to look after him and keep him supplied with boiled sweets – which he craves – and painkillers and sleeping tablets within reason. Many doctors don't want to have anything to do with a youngster in this state, so I would look elsewhere for enough sleeping pills to see him through.'

However, getting through 'cold turkey', which may take up to ten days altogether, can all too often be a waste of effort. Joan Keogh explains: 'You know that all the time they are going through this terrible suffering they also are fully aware that it will take only one smoke for the pains to begin to disappear. So they're often tempted to give up halfway through and go to the nearest pusher. There is a saying hereabouts that "heroin is easier to buy than a loaf of bread", and that is why we are insisting that we need a residential centre for our kids – it's too difficult for them to try to break the habit on their own with temptation all around them.'

Once it is known that a child is a user, the drug culture becomes part of the parent's lifestyle. It could even be argued that parents are better off not knowing, unless they can do something to help. But the fact is that no one can do anything effective until the addict has reached the point where his motivation to give up drugs is strong enough for him to stand a chance of success.

Joan Keogh found that the drug problem took over her life: 'When I remember the peace of mind I had before I knew my sons were on drugs, I ask myself what knowing about them has meant for me. The boys haven't changed – they're still on drugs. The only person to change is me – I've been through hell, but I must be fairly tough. I do think that being working-class can mean that you have more going for you when things get rough. First there was the heartbreak and desolation. Then I soon found these feelings turning to anger. I knew I had to go out there and do something to smash the pusher system and get treatment for our kids.'

To go 'out there' to do battle with the pushers and campaign for treatment facilities was precisely what Joan Keogh did, only to find that her first task was to try to convince the powers that be in her area that there *was* a serious drug problem.

PADA had been in existence for fifteen months, with a membership of about 200 and a 16-strong working-party, when I visited the Wirral. Increasing co-operation with the police and success in the group's campaign for tougher sentencing when drug-pushers are brought to trial have led to a reduction in the number of known drug-pushers from 30 or 40 to only two, it has been claimed. However, this progress has not been matched by a corresponding reduction in the number of young addicts, and the pushers that remain seem more than capable of meeting the demand.

So how serious is the problem in the Wirral?

'People ask for statistics, but it is very difficult to be precise,' says Mrs Keogh. 'It is true to say that it is harder to find youngsters who are *not* on drugs in this area than those who are. In two roads alone in one housing estate I have counted a total of twelve male addicts aged from seventeen to 21 years. Their parents are well aware of their addiction because nearly all of them have served one or two prison sentences, and have stolen from their own parents. In the last two months, 150 boys and girls have been arrested for drug offences on the Woodchurch Housing Estate alone. And we know that in the north end of Birkenhead there are families with three or four youngsters on drugs, and some of them are as young as nine or ten years of age.'

Because so many of the parents in the Merseyside area had sons who were addicted, it would be easy to get the impression that girls were to some extent immune to the deadly lure of heroin. This is not the case. Indeed, in Joan Keogh's conversations with schoolchildren throughout the area, girls often tended to express more interest in drugs, and exhibit more knowledge of them, than boys.

'You must realize,' she told me, 'that I'm learning all the time, and I suppose I will always know more about the painful end results than about the drugs themselves. For instance, when I visited a Liverpool school recently, the kids told me they were on solvents and butane gas and something called amyl nitrate, which I'd never heard of before. They said this is supposed to enhance sexual experience, and you can buy a supply for £2 at the corner sex shop!'

'The nightmare experience of having a teenage girl on hard drugs is like everything you've ever read in a sensational newspaper account and worse,' explained the mother of Jean, from a well-to-do family in the Home Counties. Jean began experimenting with 'soft' drugs while at boarding school, and got hooked on heroin during a summer vacation in Zurich when she was sixteen. Now 21, she has beaten the habit and seems safely launched on a satisfying career, but not before she had witnessed the death of a close friend under the influence of drugs and alcohol.

'She was a total wreck for more than a year,' her mother recalls. 'I'll never forget our first sight of her after she returned from what we had assumed to be a perfectly respectable holiday with friends in Switzerland. In place of the fussy and fastidious girl she had been, the person who came back was unspeakably filthy and foul-mouthed, wretchedly thin and pale, and certainly mentally disturbed and disoriented. It transpired that she had left the friends she was visiting and had moved on to Amsterdam to live in a squat with some foreign students she had met. Frankly I think she was out of her depth from the start in this hippie-style culture, but she clearly got carried away by the novelty of it all. As she seems to have been half stoned most of the time she was with this group she couldn't – or wouldn't – tell us much about how they managed to live and pay for drugs. And to tell the truth we were afraid to probe too deeply.'

The miracle, as her mother sees it, was that Jean found her way home, when her boyfriend returned to the United States. Her appearance was such a shock that there was no time for anger or cross-examination. 'The main thing was that she was home safely,' her mother admitted, 'and there was plenty to do to try to restore her to a clean and fit state, and get some nourishment into her.'

'At first Jean was so frail and lifeless that she was easy enough to manage. She hadn't eaten properly for a long time, so we were able to feel that we were achieving something by feeding her up with good food and extra vitamins. We were also able to pay for some private psychiatric help for her, though we are not sure that this did much good because the first thing she did when she was better was to go out and find a drug dealer.

'After this she was terribly unpredictable for a long time. She would seem to have beaten the habit for a week or two and then, without warning, she would disappear for several days. Once she didn't return for several weeks, and we didn't know what to do. We were on the point of reporting her missing when she turned up again, looking pretty rough, but never as bad as that first time. It took at least 18 months before we could feel that she was beating the habit at last. The turning point came when she fell in love with a nice young man who had never been involved with drugs but understood her problems. I think he gave her back her self-respect.'

One of the most important factors contributing to drug abuse among young people, according to professionals in the field, is 'peer group' involvement. The temptation to experiment is almost irresistible if all your friends are users and, consequently, have no other interests. A common characteristic among addicted teenagers is an absence of relationships with members of the opposite sex, Mike's mother remarked.

'You used to have a girlfriend for a while. You used to go to discos and you even played football at one time, but that was before you got into drugs,' she reminded her son.

'Aye, I did,' he agreed glumly.

'He doesn't have time or energy for anything like that now. Drugs are his whole life,' she summed up.

In Joan Keogh's view, even youngsters who experiment with glue-sniffing and 'soft' drugs while they are at school stand a much better chance of avoiding addiction if they have a boy-friend or girlfriend in their early teens and can find a job.

'If it is so obvious that all you need do to protect youngsters is to make sure that they have other interests which keep them out of temptation's way – away from where the drugs are – it should be possible to devise an effective preventive programme.' But, she added, this would take a lot more social awareness and willingness than exists at present.

In its short life, PADA has certainly made the problem of drug abuse in the Wirral known to a large local and national audience, and already it has made some progress in the achievement of its three principal aims: to campaign for a residential detoxification centre for the area; to establish a parents' support and information centre; and to perform an educational role.

Co-operation with parent-teacher groups has facilitated visits to schools throughout Merseyside, so that PADA members can tell pupils about the grim reality of drug abuse. They feel that if someone with first-hand experience could have spoken 'straight from the heart' to their own children in time, they might at least have thought about what they were doing when first offered heroin. More recently, the local council gave the group an empty shop at a low rent which will be used as an information centre for parents. However, raising funds for as major a project as a residential centre obviously presents a greater difficulty, and the group is hoping that an Urban Aid grant will be forthcoming.

No one would pretend that it is easy for a group of parents to muster their energies and court publicity in this fight for their children's lives, which inevitably means coping with private anguish in the face of public scrutiny. Understandably, parents who have suffered so much torment feel hurt and bewildered to find their judgement questioned by professionals who, in the words of one parent, 'think they know better'. After all, leading doctors are increasingly supporting the view that those who live with the affected child day in, day out, are the real professionals where developmental problems are concerned.

'Always listen to what the parents have to say,' child specialists advise when lecturing to students. But at the same time it is not possible to announce that a particular area has an overwhelming drugs problem without implying, however unfairly, that someone in a position of responsibility has been remiss in not recognizing it sooner. And so, officials tend to react defensively and sometimes with apparent hostility.

This was indeed the experience of Joan Keogh and her fellow PADA members.

'I had never imagined that I would find myself involved in public speaking or in arguments with officials, and I would be far happier if it hadn't been necessary,' admitted Joan Keogh. 'I remember that when we started the group we were very pleased to have council involvement, but a lot of parents broke away because they thought meetings were developing into a talking shop with too much jargon and too little in the way of practical ideas. For a start we had to convince the council that we had a problem; it was only through publicity that we did convince them.'

When the borough council set up a Drug Abuse Panel, Mrs Keogh was appointed to represent parents – an experience which she found frustrating.

'There I was, the only parent among a group of high-powered officials, and I didn't know what they were talking about. Moreover, they didn't seem to listen to a word I said. From the beginning we were saying that we needed a residential centre, but the professionals insisted that this wasn't necessary – that young addicts can give up drugs with counselling help, while they are living at home.

'By this time, some of the group's youngsters had been on hard drugs for up to four years, and we knew they couldn't manage to kick the habit on their own while living at home, because it had been tried over and over again. We all know the routine you have to try to follow once an addict decides that he wants to stop. First, you have to get to him immediately before he changes his mind. Then you have to try to stay with him, to nurse him for days and days through the withdrawal symptoms and keep him separated from his friends and sources of supply. Even then you've only a slight hope that it will work this time, without a supportive residential environment.'

Far from feeling demoralized at the low success rate they have witnessed so far in tackling heroin addiction, PADA members are sustained by the belief that a carefully designed residential programme could restore their children to a normal way of life. But they know only too well that any treatment programme will be fraught with difficulties.

'Apart from the programme at Prestwich Hospital, Manchester, which can take time and perhaps several stays – and where they have only a small number of beds – I haven't come across any form of professional help which has proved really useful,' Mrs Keogh said. 'I know one young man who has made a great success of getting himself off heroin without any help by doing "cold turkey", but he is highly motivated, and he gets the strength and stimulation he needs through his involvement with Narcotics Anonymous [NA]. Quite a number of older lads have managed to kick the habit on their own with the help of NA, but it's more difficult when you're dealing with younger kids.'

PADA members know what kind of residential detoxification and rehabilitation centre they need because such centres exist in various parts of Britain. They are equally sure that the wrong kind of residential provision could do more harm than good. In one such case a youth being admitted to hospital was kept waiting in a geriatric ward's dayroom for an entire day. He was treated contemptuously by some nursing staff, and was so free of any disciplinary constraints that a pusher visited him to supply heroin. The pusher was also able to attend a hospital disco.

On the other hand, some programmes can be too exacting, they claim. One centre in Lancaster with a high success rate uses behaviour therapy involving a 'token' system of rewards for compliance. This treatment demands a higher level of motivation more than many younger addicts can muster. For instance, a young man from the Wirral found he could not bring himself to comply with one entrance requirement, which was to shout at the top of his voice, 'I am a drug addict and I need help,' even though he had stood up to a long and rigorous interview.

Some parents feel that programmes which rely too heavily on self-discipline are too tough for many teenage addicts. One new detoxification unit based in a local hospital has an out-patient programme which includes twice-weekly visits for psychiatric counselling. At other times a nurse visits the patient's home to test urine samples. If there is evidence of drug abuse, then the youngster is excluded from the programme.

'I told them that this scheme was doomed to failure even before it started,' said Joan Keogh. 'It is due to cost £73,000 over a three-year period, but we know from experience that a programme of this kind makes it too difficult for youngsters to manage without close supervision. There was a big response initially and they had quite a big waiting list, but youngsters tended to drop out when they saw how little personal support they were getting.'

Talking to parents had certainly convinced me that much more needs to be done for young people who find themselves involved in drug abuse. But to get a clearer picture of the problem as seen from the viewpoint of those with responsibility for the welfare of young people in the area, I talked to Tom Curran, deputy director of social services for Wirral Borough Council.

According to the official view, there is as yet no hard evidence that parents in the Wirral have to contend with a more serious drug abuse problem than parents in many other parts of Britain. So why single out the Wirral for special attention? The answer is simple. As the preceding pages show, it is clear that the area has a problem. And we know about it because Wirral parents decided to 'come out' and share something of their heartbreak, in the belief that publicity will help to find a solution to their problem. While publicity can lead to sensational misreporting and unwelcome attention, it can often work wonders, too.

It was only to be expected that Wirral social services chiefs would find some aspects of PADA's activities troublesome, not least because of the ensuing intrusion of newspaper reporters and television cameras, demanding an account of the services

31

which were available to cope with an epidemic of heroin abuse.

'What we are seeing is a very distorted picture, an exaggerated view of the facts as seen through the eyes of people who are personally concerned with the problem,' said Tom Curran. 'There are no proper statistics to show the rate of drug abuse among adolescents in the area. The only figures available are those for attendance at the new detoxification unit at Arrowe Park Hospital, and the counselling centre run by the Merseyside Drugs Council at Birkenhead.

'There is no disputing the fact that heroin is an addictive drug and a potential destroyer. But we think there is a lot of confusion in the way that PADA members fail to distinguish between drug dependency, drug abuse and occasional use. In most cases the level of physical addiction from smoking heroin is much lower than by injection, and for many withdrawing on a "cold turkey" basis is not much worse than a bad bout of 'flu, for which you wouldn't need residential provision.'

Motivation on the part of the person concerned is the most important factor in any treatment programme, Mr Curran claimed in defence of the new detoxification unit's rule – that anyone with a positive urine test would be sacked from the scheme. Far from being an exceptional practice, this is often a routine condition of treatment. 'Resources are much too scarce to waste on youngsters who don't want to kick the habit,' he continued. 'If they are not motivated, it's a waste of time, and you have to wait until they are ready. But although we sympathize with parents when they think it possible to admit them to a therapeutic unit and cure them – just as simply as that – we view the problem as a community problem which is best dealt with in the community.'

According to Mr Curran, expert counselling, such as that provided through the Merseyside Drugs Council in Birkenhead, can do a lot to help a client towards reaching a frame of mind in which there is the will to kick the habit and start a new life. But counselling takes time, and there seldom are enough professional counsellors at hand to give everyone with a drug problem all the help needed. None the less, there is a great deal which parents can do to help in most cases, by joining a support group and learning how to help the child cope with the pressures of adolescence. His message to parents is 'Yes, you can do something about it'. 'The basic problem,' he claims, 'is not drugs but adolescence – with its contradictions and emotional upheaval and inconsistencies – and lack of communication. All cases of drug abuse with which I personally have come in contact have been associated with difficulties in family relationships; where parents can best help their children is in working to restore those relationships.'

Because it is now possible to smoke heroin, this has become increasingly a drug of abuse, but it is essential to look at this problem in the context of other forms of addiction which to a great extent are socially acceptable, though far more destructive in the long term. There are far more people abusing alcohol, for instance, than there used to be; and the typical alcohol-abuser tends to be an older family man with responsibilities which are adversely affected by his addiction. By contrast, the average drug-abuser is young and single.

When local welfare resources where one would hope to find help with a specific problem are in short supply, parents with an affected child may well conclude that little or nothing is being done by the authorities in the area. Perhaps in their great personal anguish they tend to lose sight of the enormous responsibilities which local authority social services departments have for children, the elderly, handicapped, mentally ill and homeless people, and that there is seldom enough money to go round.

But Mr Curran stressed that far from ignoring the growing problem of drug abuse, the Wirral Borough Council has a broadly based strategy for dealing with it, which has been developed over a period of time.

'The authority's education department takes a very responsible stance on this question,' he explained. 'We hold parent-teacher meetings; we run courses for teachers in primary and secondary schools; we distribute information packs so that all schools in the Wirral have a very good information service. At the same time we are very conscious of the need for care; of the argument that to go beyond a certain point in discussing drugs may even encourage youngsters to experiment.'

The problem of solvent abuse among younger children (one

33

which many parents see as having led to drug abuse in their own children) has been studied thoroughly by the authority's researchers. The term 'solvent abuse' is preferable to 'glue-sniffing', according to Mr Curran. 'One of our discoveries was that there is very little glue-sniffing as such, but there is a lot of solvent abuse. We have identified about 64 different substances, including butane gas and hair-spray, which youngsters in the area have been using. You can buy these from chemists and DIY stores, so we have been discussing the problem with shopkeepers and the British Sealants Association, which is the manufacturers' representative body. We have a counsellor who gives talks to youngsters, and individual counselling sessions are also available.'

There may not be much hope of PADA achieving its ambition of having its own residential therapeutic centre for local young people in the next year or so. But its members must surely feel encouraged by some of the developments which are planned for 1985 in the Wirral.

In addition to the Inner Area Programme which is already providing funds for the employment of six counsellors, Wirral Social Services Department is opening a 'crash-pad' facility which will provide five beds each with a maximum of five nights' occupation for youngsters taking drugs.

'The idea of the crash-pad is that we have a place where they can stay for a limited period. This will give us a chance to talk to them, assess their level of motivation, and find out if they are interested in kicking the habit,' explained Mr Curran.

Secondary accommodation to which well-motivated youngsters willing to enter into a contract can transfer from the crash-pad is also scheduled, consisting of a residential unit to provide bedsitter facilities for twelve residents for up to six months. The authority is funding this, in co-operation with a voluntary housing association.

Yet another good omen for the Wirral is the news that the pioneering American organization Phoenix House plans to set up a therapeutic unit for up to 50 residents, with funding from the Department of Health and Social Security. Phoenix House, which already has branches in London, Sheffield and South Tyneside, has a reputation for success in the treatment of drug abuse based upon its principles of behaviour modification and reinforcement strategies.

Planning services is never easy without precise information with regard to the number of people needing care. To ascertain the true extent of drug abuse in the Wirral – especially among adolescents – the authority is funding a two-year action-research programme, which is being undertaken by the department of social science at Liverpool University. As far as future trends are concerned, Mr Curran takes an optimistic view, believing that the current preoccupation ·with drug abuse will pass – as so many other adolescent problems have done in their time.

Meanwhile, though no one is suggesting that developments in the Wirral have been prompted or expedited by campaigning pressures from groups such as PADA, it is tempting to speculate that someone's prayers are being answered.

3 Where is the child I used to know?

How would you know if your child was using drugs?

Experts say you should watch out for changes in behaviour rather than any physical signs. As parents who have been through the experience testify, drug abuse tends to be an insidious development in the early stages. There is rarely one particular day which they could single out in retrospect and of which they could say, 'That was the day my child began using drugs'. Yet there are changes in mood and attitude which they can often remember noticing, once it is known that a child is using solvents or drugs. The changes are usually subtle to begin with, and it may only be when a pattern of altered behaviour emerges that parents finally suspect that something is wrong.

Research has shown that parents, in fact, notice a great deal without realizing that there is any cause for concern. This was shown in notable studies carried out in the 1960s by two psychiatrists in Crawley New Town; Dr N.H. Rathod and Dr R. de Alarcón, whose findings were reported in the *Lancet* in 1967 and in the *British Medical Journal* in 1968. With the aim of discovering 'oddities of behaviour and appearance' which parents had noticed before the use of drugs came to light, a group of twenty parents of heroin-users were asked for information. The results of the studies were as follows:

80 per cent – lack of appetite;

70 per cent – no interest in personal appearance;

65 per cent – unexpected absences from home (to obtain supply);

65 per cent – long periods spent in his room;

65 per cent – sleeps out (loses motivation to come home when high);

60 per cent – slow and halting speech;

60 per cent – gives up organized activities;

55 per cent – receives and makes frequent telephone calls (to check on supplies);

45 per cent – blood spotting on clothes (mainly pyjama tops and shirts);

45 per cent – litter in room or pockets;

45 per cent – stooped posture;

20 per cent – burnt matches lying around (e.g. floating in toilet bowl);

15 per cent – teaspoons lying around (used to prepare 'fix').

Once the Crawley parents began to attend group meetings, they became much more alert to telltale behaviour changes in their children. In two cases suspicions were to prove correct when a sudden loss of appetite for breakfast was noted, and when a resumption of frequent telephone calls followed a more leisurely drug-free period.

A tendency to make new friends, and lose contact with existing companions, may well be a sign of healthy development in adolescence, and the cultivation of new interests may be entirely desirable. On the other hand it could also mean that contact is being limited to companions who share an interest in drugs, and that the new friends involved in frequent telephone calls are actually drug-pushers.

At the same time, parents have to realize that many of the signs listed in any drugs checklist are also commonly associated with normal adolescent behaviour: moodiness, bouts of depression, self-doubt, episodes of stubbornness, rejection of authority, and so on. Moreover, emotional problems entirely unrelated to drugs can interfere with appetite and cause symptoms of anxiety. Perhaps the young person is worrying about an examination or an interview or about finding money for some perfectly acceptable purchase. Disappointment in love or friendship or in a family relationship could also cause emotional upset. Young people need freedom to develop, to make their own choices and mistakes. There are times when adult intervention is neither useful nor welcome.

Nevertheless, as the Crawley researchers warned doctors, 'If many of these signs occur together, and there have been recent changes in general behaviour, drug dependence should be high on the list' of possible explanations. These researches are discussed in *Drugs* (Penguin, 1971) by Peter Laurie, who goes on to describe the painstaking piece of medical detective work undertaken by Dr de Alarcón in order to track down the pattern of heroin initiation in Crawley from 1962 to '65. Through interviews with users he was able to show that it had begun with a few Crawley teenagers being introduced to the drug in other towns: 32 users were traced to one contact in Worthing, and 16 to one contact in Brighton.

From this study it was deduced that drug initiation was a process which took place in the main between friends who trusted each other, rather than a case of cheap or free samples being offered by a pusher. At the time, heroin was very much scarcer and a great deal more expensive than it is in Britain in the mid-1980s. Young people are still being initiated into heroin abuse by friends. But today it is easier than ever to establish and maintain contact with pushers, especially in smaller towns where clients and pushers are likely to live in the same housing estates.

'Sure, everyone gets the first fix free, whether it's from a friend or a pusher. Then you start paying until it costs you everything that meant anything to you in the days before you got hooked,' warned a recovering addict. 'Someone should be out there telling the kids that there's no such thing as a free fix.'

Today, when smoking heroin is so much more common than injecting among younger users, the telltale signs to watch out for include an interest in everyday household items which are needed for smoking. Tinfoil to hold the powder while it is being heated to give off fumes, matches and firm paper which can be rolled into a tube to draw up the fumes into the mouth, are among the required basics. Needless to say, discarded tubes, burnt tinfoil and spent matches are more or less conclusive evidence, if these are left lying around and parents know enough to be suspicious.

Pauline's son's apparently sudden and peculiar interest in discarded household packaging was the pointer which eventually alerted her to his heroin abuse.

'In the beginning it was all a bit of a joke,' she remembers. 'He was particularly keen on getting cartons from a certain brand of tea, which had foil on the inside. He never said anything – I just noticed that he was purloining them and I got curious first . . . then I had this niggling worry because other things were coming to my notice, too. Looking back I could see that his whole way of life had changed for the worse over the previous few months. When I finally cornered him for a straight answer, he was quick enough to own up that he was on drugs.'

For Carol the first inkling that all was not well with her schoolboy son was his increasing untidiness and unaccustomed litter in his previously tidy bedroom. The giveaway clues were a mirror and a packet of razor blades which she found in a drawer one day when she was tidying his room.

'When you have someone who is not even old enough to shave regularly, and doesn't take the slightest interest in his appearance, finding something like that gives you a weird feeling – you are aware that it isn't natural, somehow,' Carol remembers. 'Now I know that the mirror provides a reflective surface so that he doesn't miss a grain when he "cuts" the heroin powder into small rations with the razor blade.'

Carol believes that sometimes parents seem to realize that something is wrong long before they will admit it even to themselves. 'I think you can go on for ages trying to reassure yourself and burying your head in the sand. You read so many scary newspaper reports, and you tell yourself that this isn't a bit like my son. But deep down I think now that I did know and didn't want to face up to it. For one thing he had changed so much – lounging around and doing nothing, whereas he used to be so energetic and he was also an avid reader. I think what clinched it was finding these neat little folds of paper torn from glossy magazines. I now know that pushers use these to package the heroin.'

One of the first worrying signs of changing behaviour which Carol had noticed was a deterioration in her son's school reports which she put down to temporary loss of interest at an awkward stage of adolescence. She suggests that early changes in attitude and behaviour associated with drug use may sometimes be more clearly apparent during school hours than in the more relaxed atmosphere of the home. According to Carol this is where closer parent-teacher contacts, not only through formal meetings but

39

by means of the occasional 'quiet word', could be very helpful.

We know from parents how helpful teachers can be in alerting them to the possibility of drug use among their children. Clearly, teachers see a side of the child which parents seldom get a chance to observe. Even in large classes, the child who seems to have undergone a sudden change in personality cannot fail to be conspicuous. Unruly behaviour and unexpected rudeness in a previously co-operative child, unaccustomed lethargy or excitability, loss of interest in school work and sports, frequent absences without explanation – all of these, according to Brian, a sixth-form teacher, can build up into a pattern of behaviour which suggests something more than ordinary teenage rebelliousness.

'The trouble is that it's not always easy to tell when a child's difficulties are due to drugs,' Brian pointed out. 'You are noticing changes in behaviour all the time in children of this age, and obviously it's not always possible to do very much about it. As often as not, the trouble is temporary and is due to some problem at home. Perhaps someone in the family is ill, or there is danger of the parents splitting up, or the family has debts and money is very scarce. The fact that there are no jobs for most of today's school-leavers encourages a feeling of helplessness and powerlessness and hopelessness. This is the sort of situation where drugs seem to offer an escape . . .'

Even when a teacher has strong suspicions that a child is involved in solvent or drug abuse it is not usually easy to broach the subject with parents. Brian explained: 'I would have to be pretty sure before I would suggest to a parent that a child might be taking drugs. Not long ago we had a boy who turned up in class looking unsteady on his feet. When I looked at his eyes I saw that his pupils were narrowed down to pinpoint size. So I was able to say, "Come on, I know you've been taking drugs – tell me about it." He admitted that he had been smoking heroin, so we were able to arrange for an educational welfare officer to visit his parents.'

The need for a realistic level of communication between parents and teachers is greater than ever, now that drug use has become so prevalent among adolescents. But for it to be successful both sides must get rid of some of their inhibitions,

Brian explained: 'If a parent asks me a direct question about an unruly child's behaviour, I hope I will have the strength of mind in future to tell the whole truth, now that I see such an increase in drug use locally. In the past when I could see that a parent was desperately anxious not to get a bad report, I would find myself tending to soften the blow and make excuses. Call it weakness, if you like. I think we will have to be much more outspoken in future, in the children's interests, and I hope parents can understand this.'

The signs are that a more open attitude is already developing, as the message spreads that drugs are a menace to all our children, whatever our circumstances or lifestyle. One of the benefits of recent publicity is that parents now realize that they are not alone, that they are not to blame, and that there are even likely to be a great many other parents with a similar problem in their own immediate neighbourhood.

Not very long ago, there was probably no one to talk to if you discovered that your child was abusing drugs. You just suffered in silence in an agony of shame and apprehension, assuming that everyone was blaming you for being a bad parent. Worse still, you might well be the last person to find out that your child was involved with drugs because it was not the sort of news that anyone would wish to pass on to a parent. Indeed, something of this attitude still remains.

In the hope of preventing a slide into more serious dependence, professionals stress the importance of recognizing drug abuse among young people at as early a stage as possible. Obviously, it is very difficult for parents to identify a problem early on because of the large number of their waking hours which children spend away from home. Yet all too often it is only through a slow and painful realization that all is not well that parents become aware that their child is using drugs.

As can be seen from the accounts given by parents in this book, changes in behaviour usually provide the first clues: the teenage boy with a passion for outdoor sport who now spends most of his spare time in his bedroom; the brightest girl in the class who has suddenly become an under-achiever; the ambitious youngster who never talks about the future nowadays. One of the most conspicuous changes is, of course, a sudden desperate need for more and more money to support the habit, without anything tangible to show for the extra expenditure.

Bob is a widower with a teenage son and a daughter of twenty. He blames himself for not noticing certain changes in his son's routine which should have prompted him to ask questions, although he was away at work all day.

'The first thing I should have noticed was that he had been much quieter than usual for several months – no more blaring pop music throbbing out from the record-player that used to be his pride and joy, for instance; no pop music programmes on the radio, for that matter; no bicycle; no sports equipment,' Bob remembers. 'It was only when I overheard his sister taunting him about his empty room, and not wanting any more of her things "walking out the back door" that I knew something was badly wrong.'

According to Bob, it is only too easy to miss telltale clues when you are leading a busy life and seeing your children only briefly in the evening. 'You want to put your feet up, have a bit of peace when you come home,' he recalls. 'Where I went wrong was in not realizing that everything was too peaceful in contrast to the bedlam I used to complain about so much . . . As far as I knew, my son was a well-behaved, studious boy who spent a lot of time in his room. What I should have noticed was that he had parted with everything of value that he had been given as birthday and Christmas presents going back many years; and he had nothing to show for it.'

While Bob blames himself bitterly, he feels nevertheless that his son's teachers must have noticed something which could have been reported back to him through the school's health service. When questioned, they said that the boy was only one of many whose attitude and general behaviour seemed to change during adolescence – a process so commonplace as to appear quite normal. He now sees a case for more frequent health checks in schools, including regular visits by a school nurse who could pay particular attention to youngsters whose behaviour is causing concern.

One of the difficulties is that no one has a duty to inform parents that a child may be abusing drugs, apart from the policeman who picks him up for theft or for being in possession of a prohibited substance. Ideally, the problem should have been identified long before it reached this stage. One answer to why this does not happen is that teenagers are quite good at covering their tracks in the early stages; that it is only later on when the habit has taken a firm hold that they become careless and tend to leave clues lying around.

Certainly, many teachers feel they have a duty to inform parents if they are convinced that a child is abusing drugs, but there are also some who may adopt a different attitude. This was explained by Lady Hornsby-Smith when she spoke in a House of Lords debate on the need for stricter laws to control traffic in drugs. She was appalled, she said, by the trendy views of some teachers and university lecturers who told her own friends, 'I couldn't possibly warn you that your boy is taking drugs. I would have lost his confidence.' Had they seen the same boy drowning, they would not have hesitated to rush to his rescue. So why, she asked, could they not have the same attitude towards the boy who might be killing himself with heroin?

However, the choices for teachers are seldom so clear-cut, especially where younger children are concerned. While education authorities have had guidelines relating to teaching about drug misuse going back many years, the task of including the subject in the curriculum has proved far from easy. It has also been suggested that to place too much emphasis on drugs and drug-taking could have the opposite of the desired effect. At a time of teacher shortage and an increasing incidence of drug abuse, there is patently an urgent need for national guidelines. It is to be hoped that the government's campaign (which is being co-ordinated by the Central Office of Information) will help to meet this need.

In the Scottish Health Education Unit's booklet for teachers and others working with young people (*Drugs and Young People in Scotland*, 1977), authors Dr A.B. Ritson and Dr M.A. Plant point out that 'it is extremely easy to conceal drug-taking and difficult to separate drug effects from other adolescent ups and downs'. They also warn against focusing attention on the drug rather than the person using it, especially as the fear of expul-

43

sion from school or some other form of punishment could drive the child into further secrecy and an unwillingness to seek help from adults when it is needed.

'The first essential, when an adult suspects someone of taking drugs, is to try to gain their confidence so that the young person will talk sufficiently frankly to place the extent and seriousness of the drug used within the context of their total life,' the authors advise. 'It is important to help and support the young person in trouble, not to penalize or harass him or her. This should be an important consideration when deciding to whom one turns for help. Advice should be sought from people who will treat drug misusers confidentially and sympathetically . . . In some areas there are drug liaison committees or specialized treatment services which can offer advice.'

While this line of advice can apply equally well to parents as well as teachers, difficulties are more likely to arise when it is the teacher who gains a young person's confidence on the basis that parents will not be told without the pupil's consent. Such knowledge can impose a heavy burden on a teacher who is not in a position to undertake responsibility for the young person's welfare, or even to observe his or her behaviour most of the time.

Lady Hornsby-Smith is obviously in no doubt as to the correct course to follow in this sort of situation. However, for the individual teacher the ethical issues may not be so easily resolved. One way out of this dilemma would be for teachers to discourage confidences of this kind, so that they can feel freer to report any suspicions to parents. But would this be a better way to help the child who finds it easier to confide in a teacher? Are there not times when quiet counselling by a respected teacher may be the best form of treatment?

What would most parents want in these circumstances? No doubt many would say that they had a right to know anything affecting their child's wellbeing which was known to another adult. Others, in the light of agonizing experience, would argue that parents are better off not knowing about the problem until the young person is ready to attempt a 'cure'. On the other hand, it seems highly desirable that parents should have insight into the background affecting their child's behaviour and general health, and especially so in case of any emergency such as an overdose.

Can your child's personality or temperament provide clues as to a possible vulnerability to the temptation of drug misuse? While it seems to be generally agreed that there is no such thing as an 'addictive personality', vulnerability is another matter. At the other extreme from the breezy, outgoing youngster who is very much one of the gang and willing to try anything at least once, there is the lonely youngster, lacking self-confidence and friends, for whom solvent-sniffing or drugs may seem to offer a way of escape. Doctors advise that children in this category need extra attention. Perhaps they get less attention than they need because they are less demanding than their more robust brothers and sisters.

Several parents have volunteered the view that, in their own families, the child with the drug problem tended to be 'kinder, more thoughtful, less self-centred, less aggressive' than brothers or sisters who had never been tempted to use drugs. 'This is a very common experience,' said a member of Families Anonymous. 'Some parents also find that the child who became addicted had always tended to be more artistic and more gifted in other ways, too. I'm not suggesting that all artistic or gifted youngsters are at risk, but it must mean something when a lot of parents have a similar experience.'

'He was always gentler, more affectionate than the others. He would worry about leaving you alone in the evening, and maybe decide to stay in with you if you didn't insist that he should go out and enjoy himself,' recalls the mother of a young man who is on the way to recovery through membership of Narcotics Anonymous. 'Under the influence of drugs he changed a lot – becoming very pettish and demanding a lot of attention – but he was never aggressive. That is the only thing to be said in favour of heroin: it doesn't seem to make them aggressive.'

Some authorities are convinced that enough clues can be detected in a young person's attitude and behaviour to say whether or not he would be likely to use drugs, given the opportunity.

According to Dr Armand M. Nicholi Jnr. of Massachusetts

General Hospital and Harvard Medical School (*World Health Forum*, Vol. 5, 1984) people who use illicit drugs differ markedly from non-users. 'Large-scale studies with a high degree of reliability have shown that there are important differences in attitude and values, in personality traits, in home and school environment, in relations with parents and friends and in overall behaviour. The patterns of disaffection and rebellion that characterized users in the counter-culture of the 1960s continue to characterize those who use drugs today.'

He goes on to argue that, for example, regular marijuana users place a lower value on academic success and a higher value on independence than non-users. As a group they tend to be more rebellious, have more depressed moods and have low self-esteem. 'Those who use drugs even as young teenagers tend to have friends who are markedly incompatible with their parents, and tend to be more influenced by these friends than by their parents.'

The same applies to early alcohol abuse, too. Drawing upon a considerable volume of local research, the authors of *Drugs and Young People in Scotland* conclude that, for the majority of young people, using illicit drugs is very much part of the same pattern of behaviour which includes smoking and drinking. 'Most young people only get deeply involved with drug-taking if they have few interests elsewhere . . . A high proportion of young drug casualties have many other problems such as homelessness and unemployment, and have previously been in trouble with the police.'

For one police observer in an area with a high rate of juvenile drug abuse in the mid-1980s the phrase 'few interests elsewhere' sums up one of the most threatening situations for working-class teenagers.

'The tragedy is that while the opportunities to experiment are available equally to all sections of society, the risks are highest for youngsters in poorer areas because they tend to have few of the resources which prevent better-off kids from becoming casualties.

'Of course you do find casualties among middle-class youngsters, and large numbers use drugs for a time – maybe even occasionally over a long period. Where the main difference lies is in the fact that they usually have plenty of other interests and a social structure to their lives, which enables them to keep their drug-taking within certain limits. The same applies to upper-class young people who think it's just good fun to take a snort of cocaine after dinner, and they just carry on with their normal lives the rest of the time. On the other hand, for the youngster from a poorer background in which there are no other distractions, there is a much greater tendency for drugs to take over completely and become a way of life in themselves.'

Clearly, this argument makes sense. For most of us it is other interests which keep us on an even keel when something goes awry in other areas of our lives. Loss of interest in sporting activities tends to be mentioned very frequently as one of the most conspicuous changes in behaviour noticed prior to the discovery of drug misuse. But this trend is not necessarily a sign that something is amiss: many adolescents who seem good at games are only too glad to give up practice, once freed of the obligation to play in a school team.

'I think that what we need to worry about is what interests young people take up to replace those they have lost,' a city youth worker explained. 'We all have a picture in our minds of the young person whose parents don't need to worry – someone who has a regular job and a fairly set routine, who has an easy relationship with schoolmates or new friends from work, and perhaps a steady girlfriend. He spends his money on tangible purchases of some kind, and if he goes "broke" it's usually at a predictable time of the week or month. In other words, he behaves normally, but, as parents explain, "behaving normally" is far more difficult for the young person with no job, no structure to his day, no apparent purpose to his life; and perhaps one of the most vital factors of all – no discipline.

'We are hearing about more and more unemployed teenagers who are drifting into heroin abuse through the sheer boredom of having nothing to do all day,' the youth worker continued. 'If their parents are out at work, even only part-time, it means that there are long periods every day when they are left to their own devices. Let's face it – that isn't the fault of anyone in the family. In reasonable circumstances, it shouldn't be necessary to baby-sit with young men and women of their age.'

The solution, he believes, is more community support for families, of a kind which is acceptable to young people. 'I am thinking in particular of youth club activities where all sorts of interests could be stimulated, including camping weekends and so on, but with some additional element which would give parents the right to seek a place for a vulnerable teenager. As it is, we never see the youngsters who most need our help at youth clubs: once they are into drug use they just don't bother to come along. I suppose what I'm really saying is that I would like to see some form of gentle compulsion, rather on the lines of the Intermediate Treatment youth programme operating through social services departments and the courts. But the biggest stumbling-block of all is that at present we haven't got enough money for facilities, even if young people were willing to use them.'

When, as occasionally happens, parents are criticized for not having more control over teenagers, one very important factor tends to be forgotten. This is the extent to which parental authority is normally backed up by school and later by the discipline essential to paid employment. By contrast, parents of unemployed teenagers have to manage completely on their own without outside support, unless through some misfortune the youngster gets into trouble with the law. Yet we still hear some doctors expressing an opinion in the best 'blame the victim' tradition that 'teenage drug abuse is neither a medical problem nor a social problem, but a problem of parental discipline . . .' On the other hand, a more compassionate view has it that most juvenile delinquency stems from an attempt to generate fun and excitement in an otherwise empty life.

Needless to say, parents have a very important role to play in providing an example and guidance, as well as being on the alert for danger signals. However, the parental task is seldom an easy one, as was shown in the Scottish Health Education Unit's 1979 report, *Ten-to-fourteen-year-olds and alcohol*, which found that nearly nine out of ten Scottish children had tasted alcohol at least once by the age of fourteen years. Though the study showed that children tended to drink less where their parents exercise a higher level of control, this should not be taken to mean that children should be forbidden to drink, warned the author of the report, Dr P.P. Aitken of Strathclyde University: 'Parents who exert very strict control over drinking run the risk of their children engaging in clandestine drinking activities.'

According to Dr Nicholi, where parents smoke, drink or use drugs, their adolescent children are likely to be more prone to illicit drug use: 'Research has shown that the absence of a parent through death, divorce or a time-demanding job contributes to many forms of emotional disorder, especially the anger, rebelliousness, low self-esteem, depression and anti-social behaviour that characterize drug-users.'

Dr Nicholi was speaking about the United States, where over half the children under 18 years (approximately 13 million children) live in a home with one or both parents missing. (In Britain, according to the National Council for One-Parent Families, about one child in every 7 or 8 (a total of 1,600,000 children) lives in a one-parent family; and the largest proportion of these families is headed by divorced women.)

In addition, Dr Nicholi observes that changes in child-rearing practice and family stability in the United States have tended to shift responsibility for child care from parents to other agencies. He also makes the startling claim backed up by 'cross-cultural studies' that English and American parents spend less time with their children than 'parents in any other nation in the world'. (Obviously, family life can never be as close in a highly structured industrialized society as it is elsewhere.)

No matter how much time parents manage to spend with their children, there comes a time when the bonds have to be loosened to allow adolescent development. The teenager should be sufficiently aware of his own rights to recognize that he is entitled to a certain respect and consideration as an individual. It is highly desirable that he should be sufficiently self-assertive to make his own judgements, express opinions, make choices, be able to say yes or no and mean it, in the face of temptation and persuasion from others.

It is unrealistic to imagine that parents can allow adolescents the time, 'space' and personal freedom demanded so insistently at this stage and still be able to monitor their behaviour and friendships adequately. The time-honoured advice that parents should always try to know their children's friends is a good one, though keeping up with them may put a strain on your home life, as Nick's mother explains: 'He had never been a difficult boy until he turned fifteen, and then suddenly he wanted to be out every night. There were constant battles about the time he came in and getting him up for school in time in the morning, and we never quite knew where he was going when he went out. Then one day a neighbour said, "I'm afraid your Nick seems to be getting in with a wild bunch of kids – I know that one of them was up in court for joy-riding in a stolen car."

'We thought it best to say nothing to Nick for the time being, while we tried to see if there was something we could do to improve matters. When he was younger his friends were always encouraged to visit him at home and they would play together happily for hours. But this stopped as he got older, for the obvious reason that they felt inhibited and self-conscious trying to chat with one or other of his parents present.

'Now, in view of what our neighbour said, it seemed terribly important that we should try to get closer to the boy, and get to know his current set of friends. We still had the problem of providing a room where they could be on their own, because our house isn't very big. In the end his father came up with what turned out to be the best solution. This was to switch bedrooms round so that the largest one could be furnished as a bedsitting-room for Nick.

'He was all for the idea once we explained that we thought he was entitled to a bit more privacy, now that he was older. We said we hoped he would feel free to entertain his friends, and that we would interfere as little as possible, so long as they behaved reasonably. At first he continued to go out most evenings but, as he began to make himself more at home in *his* room, we could see that the general arrangement was bringing much more stability into his life.

'We worried quite a lot about drugs, as a matter of fact, especially during a phase when they were always dashing off to pop concerts. There were occasions when we thought we could smell something burning which we thought might be cannabis, but they smoked quite a variety of cigarettes anyway. We decided that it wouldn't be a good idea for us to start warning about drugs, in case it gave them ideas, so we never said anything.

'When they all finally settled down into jobs, we decided that it had been well worth while struggling with all those cups of coffee, all that noisy music, the heating bills and occasional pandemonium. We probably did worry too much at the outset. Perhaps Nick was never in serious danger. But then when I hear about the problems that parents are having now because of drugs, I'm not so sure.'

All is well that ended well in this case, and it is difficult to imagine that the well-adjusted young man their son has become could ever have given his parents a serious cause for worry. Yet they had found themselves in a situation which is not in the least unusual today. It is impossible to tell in retrospect whether the parents' intervention was an essential factor in the young person's development in this case, but many experts would agree with their cautious approach to the question of possible drug misuse (which they never did get round to discussing with their son).

For obvious reasons, one of the most difficult tasks for parents is knowing how to be on the alert for danger signals in teenagers who are not known to be using drugs. Should you be watching for signs that your children are misusing drugs? A straightforward reply to this question was given by consultant psychiatrist Dr Alexander Mitchell in *WHERE on Drugs*, a parents' handbook edited by Beryl McAlhone and published by the Advisory Centre for Education (ACE) in 1971 (not in print).

'The answer is definitely "No" for three reasons,' Dr Mitchell advises: 'There are, in fact, no clear-cut signs. Any evidence that a young person is misusing drugs may be confused with the natural disturbances of adolescence – the rapid shifts of mood, the dreamy preoccupation, the irritability, the restlessness and so on.

'The second reason is a matter of trust. Adolescence is a time when, despite how they behave or what they may say, young people need to feel that their parents trust them, and that they in turn can trust their parents. If young people become aware of parental scrutiny, especially if it is surreptitious, they react in a hostile way . . .

'The third reason is to do with expectancy. We react to others' expectations of us, and tend to behave in ways in which we imagine they believe we are going to behave . . . The young person thinks, "Well, if that's how they expect me to behave, I'll damn well behave that way." The unconscious aspect of this is that the young person can then blame the parents and largely disavow his responsibility for his actions.'

According to Dr Mitchell what you should be doing, instead of watching for possible signs of drug misuse, is to work at improving communication and relationships between yourself and your teenage children. 'The way some people talk, you would think that adolescents belonged to some foreign race with whom it is impossible to communicate. This is only true if you make the mistake of being patronizing and talking down to them or, what is worse, taking up a rigid, inflexible position of adult superiority.'

Initiating discussions with teenagers on the subject of drugs requires a certain degree of caution. 'To start with, parents need to be well-informed about drugs of misuse – their nature and their true effects and damage. The biggest trap for us is to be found out by young people because we make unfounded or inaccurate statements.'

Adolescence is the time of life when 'the young know everything', according to an old Chinese proverb. It is not very difficult for teenagers to appear much more knowledgeable than their parents about something as topical as drug abuse, with its mysterious jargon, even where they are not tempted to experiment. Yet an effortless recital of the chemical names and street names of a list of substances does not necessarily imply any real grasp of their nature or effects.

This was the conclusion reached by researchers who carried out a series of studies among fourth-year pupils in three Wolverhampton schools in 1969, 1974 and 1979. The report, 'Knowledge and Experience of Young People Regarding Drug Abuse between 1969 and 1979' by Dr J. D. Wright and Dr L. Pearl (*British Medical Journal*, 7 March 1981), showed that despite familiarity with the names of drugs, pupils continued to display 'considerable ignorance and misunderstanding about how drugs are taken and their dangers'.

Television was stated by pupils to be their prime source of information about drugs, in each year of the survey. But most pupils believed that the strongest influences in persuading young people to begin using drugs were the example of friends and social pressures relating to behaviour within the young person's environment. The pupils included in the studies were described as 'predominantly non-drug-takers themselves'. In reply to the question, 'Do you personally know anyone taking drugs?' the proportion answering 'Yes' was 15 per cent in 1969; 23 per cent in 1974; 21 per cent in 1979.

Although the last of these three studies was conducted some years ago, it is significant that the trend towards increasing opiate abuse was already being recognized by young people in Wolverhampton. By 1979 the drugs most often mentioned were opiates (the group which includes heroin as well as synthetic opiates), in contrast to the trends in 1969 and 1974, when cannabis was the drug most frequently mentioned. Another change was that cocaine and solvents were mentioned for the first time in 1979.

There were some changes in the types of venue where pupils considered that drugs would be most likely to be on offer, too. By 1979 discos headed the list, with the street, parties, school, pubs and coffee bars listed in that order. The two places mentioned most often in 1979 as the source of drugs taken by friends and acquaintances were parties and discos. 'Most young people,' the report says, 'are introduced to drugs by people they know, rather than by strangers. Schools appear to continue over the ten years to be a less important place where drugs are offered.'

Replies to the question, 'Why do you think young people take these drugs?' also reflect some important changes in the views of pupils. In the most recent survey, 34 per cent thought the main reason was 'to feel big, show off, grow up', compared with 29 and 30 per cent respectively in earlier studies. While a similar number (22 per cent) thought drugs were taken 'for kicks, fun, to feel good' in each study, in 1979 twice as many as in 1974 gave 'to calm nerves' as one of the main reasons. On the

53

other hand, in 1979 only half as many as in 1969 (19 and 39 per cent respectively) thought drugs were taken because friends took them or to be 'trendy'. The same proportion (18 per cent) in 1974 and 1979 thought drugs were taken to relieve boredom and depression.

'Changes in society, the pop scene, medical and legal practice and mass media coverage have all influenced young people's knowledge and experience of drug-taking,' the authors conclude. 'Effective preventive measures must include a health education programme that discusses decision-making processes and a wider view of "drugs in society" . . . Drug education must be part of a wider and positively orientated health-education programme.'

It is ironical that at a time when there is more emphasis than ever before on healthy living, exercise, good nutrition and respect for the mind and body in general, a sizeable proportion of our young people are moving in the opposite direction. 'Parents, school governors and education committees should enquire about what kind, if any, of drug education is provided in schools . . . Schools, trades unions and community groups should sponsor and organize information and training courses . . . Ignorance as to the causes and consequences of drug use exists in the relevant professions as well, including the medical sector,' Michael Meacher MP says in his 1985 report, *Cold Comfort*.

Television must undoubtedly play a prominent part in providing the kind of health education needed. It is hoped that the government campaign launched in the spring of 1985 will at least give some young people cause to think.

PHYSICAL SIGNS AND SYMPTOMS OF DRUG USE

Symptoms vary according to the drug used; the amount of the drug used; personal factors such as temperament and whether an individual is accustomed to using a particular drug. Many of the symptoms might be due to a head cold. Others – such as signs of intoxication – are of the kind more commonly associated with alcohol. Loss of appetite is a common factor, which might also be due to illness or anxiety, or to being apprehensive about a forthcoming examination or interview.

The eyes are frequently mentioned when symptoms of drug or solvent abuse are discussed. Watering of the eyes is common with solvent abuse and as an early symptom of heroin withdrawal. The facility which the pupil of the eye has to contract in bright light and relax in shade can be affected by certain drugs. The classic case is that of heroin (and other opiates) where the muscle tightens up to give the appearance of 'pinpoint' pupils.

Other drugs have the opposite effect – of dilating the pupils – so that in some cases (with amphetamines) they do not contract even in bright light while an individual is under the influence of the drug. Drugs which cause dilation of the pupils include cannabis, amphetamines, barbiturates, cocaine, LSD and solvents. (Drugs used by doctors to assist in eye examination and treatment can also have this effect, so do not jump to conclusions if you see someone with temporarily dilated pupils. The same applies to dark glasses, which may be used to shield telltale eyes or for other reasons.)

Some of the signs and symptoms associated with drug use are described below.

Cannabis
Brown-stained fingers from smoking the drug; scent of burning herbs from room and clothing (combined with frequent use of air fresheners); thirst; dry throat; nausea and vomiting; dry cough; running nose; eyes reddened with dilated pupils; poor appetite, but may have craving for sweet foods; dizziness and signs of intoxication (similar to alcohol effects); clumsiness in movements; slurred speech; carelessness in dress; changes of mood (sometimes talkative and excitable but subject to anxiety and panic feelings at other times); poor concentration; changed sleeping habits (up at night and in bed during the day).

Solvents
Glue or other substances on skin or clothing; breath smelling of chemicals; redness or rash round mouth and nose; watering eyes; dilated pupils; chronic cough; loss of appetite and weight; slurred speech; unsteady gait; mood changes (including signs of intoxication such as giggling excessively or marked irritability), lack of interest in appearance; inability to concentrate.

Heroin

Lacking energy or interest; new friends; unusually drowsy at times; poor appetite; chronic constipation (as drug slows down intestinal movement); pinpoint pupils (which do not enlarge even in dim light); itchiness and skin infections; symptoms of bronchitis; watering of nose and eyes with start of withdrawal symptoms (may use dark glasses as a shield); neglect of appearance; changed behaviour (staying out late without explanation, untruthfulness, needing a lot of money, secretive about comings and goings, visibly anxious before going out owing to fear of withdrawal symptoms). Where the drug is injected, there may be blood stains on clothing, and needle marks – usually along veins in front of the elbow. Sometimes smaller 'pop marks' show that the drug is being injected superficially under the skin.

Barbiturates

Effects similar to those of alcohol, with the sedative effect sometimes being proceded by a phase in which there is temporary excitement and loss of inhibitions, as would result from taking stimulants. According to the amount of the drug taken, the symptoms can include an appearance of drunkenness; slurred speech; slow movements; a slow-down in breathing; irritability; sometimes aggressive behaviour; dilated pupils; sleepiness; deep sleep and risk of coma with high doses, and especially where alcohol is also taken.

Amphetamines

Sudden bursts of energy; bright and talkative (especially noticeable when fatigue might be expected); excitability; restlessness; tendency to over-sleep; occasional profuse perspiration; hands shaking sometimes; dry mouth and bad breath; sore, dry lips (tendency to lick lips frequently); thirst; poor appetite; dilated pupils even in bright light; sometimes a tendency to aggressive behaviour; sometimes hallucinations may occur with higher doses.

LSD

Dilated pupils may be a symptom in some cases. Flushed face;

shivering; chills; shaking of the hands and feet; cold, clammy palms; nausea and loss of appetite.

Cocaine

Immediate effects can include intense excitement; feelings of self-confidence; sexual excitement and increased energy. Other effects include dilated pupils; nausea and vomiting; anxiety; feelings of confusion and sleeplessness. Repeated sniffing of cocaine can damage the lining of the nose. Frequent use of the drug can result in cold sweats, fainting attacks, breathing difficulties, delirium and convulsions.

Overdose first aid

Usually when a drug overdose is suspected the first-aid treatment is the same as for any other unconscious person. Keep calm. Maintaining breathing is the most important life-saving consideration. Loosen clothing at neck and waist. Place the patient face-downwards in what is called the 'recovery position' (semi-prone with the head turned to one side and without a pillow). This ensures that neither the tongue nor vomited material drops back into the throat to cause suffocation. Always check that the mouth and throat are clear of food, dentures, etc. An unconscious person should never be placed on his or her back or propped upright in a chair, or given anything by mouth. Cover lightly to keep warm, but do not use a hot-water bottle. When calling for an ambulance, explain that the patient may have taken an overdose of drugs.

It can save a life – and a lot of time at the hospital – if you can identify the drug used. If the patient is conscious at any point, ask for this information. Collect any drugs or empty containers you can find and take them to the hospital with the patient. If the patient has vomited, bring along a specimen of the material in a clean container. If possible, find out the name of the patient's own doctor.

USEFUL ORGANIZATIONS AND PUBLICATIONS

Solvent abuse
Solvent Abuse Helpline; tel. 01–698 4415. (Call this number for

information on help-groups or for personal counselling. An information pack is available on request.)

A free Health Education Council leaflet is available through district health authorities or from the Health Education Council, Dept M50, 13/39 Standard Road, London NW10.

A photo-pack entitled *Solvent Abuse* costs £1 inclusive from Clive Parkinson, The Bottleshop, Duke's Playhouse, Moor Lane, Lancaster.

The National Campaign Against Solvent Abuse; tel. 01–640 2946 or 01–672 1585. This organization has been operating for three years and has fifteen different groups and provides a 24-hour information and advice service for parents and young people abusing solvents. Through regional contacts, enquirers can be put in touch with a local agency. The national director, Alan Billington, travels throughout Britain to talk to individuals and groups.

Heroin

How to Stop by Roger Duncan and the Blenheim workers, and *How to Help: a practical guide for friends and relatives of drug users* by Roger Duncan and Steve Tippell, are available at 60p each, inclusive of postage, from the Institute for the Study of Drug Dependence (ISDD), 1–4 Hatton Place, Hatton Garden, London EC1N 8ND. 0171 − 803 − 4712 , 928 1211.

Heroin and Other Opiates, a Release education leaflet, costs 60p, inclusive of postage, from the same address.

For a helpful leaflet entitled *Women and Heroin*, send a stamped addressed envelope to DAWN (Drugs, Alcohol, Women Nationally), 146 Queen Victoria Street, London EC4V 4BX.

Tranquillizers

Women and Tranquillizers, a self-help leaflet, is available (send a stamped addressed envelope) from DAWN (see address above).

Women and Tranquillizers by Celia Haddon (Sheldon Press, 1984);

The Tranquillizer Trap by Joy Melville (Fontana, 1984).
London TRANX, 17 Peel Road, Wealdstone, Middlesex; tel.
01–427 2065. (A self-help support group.)

Cannabis
Cannabis, a Release drug-education booklet, costs 15p plus 20p
postage from ISDD (see above).

Amphetamines
Amphetamines, a Release drug-education booklet, costs 25p
plus 20p postage from ISDD (see above).

4 Recognizing the enemy

The order in which the various substances are listed in this chapter is not meant to reflect their relevant importance or the prevalence of usage. There is of course great concern about the widespread use of heroin and, to a lesser extent, solvents, but estimates regarding the number of people involved in any form of drug misuse are seldom more than guesswork. Nor is it possible to predict what the pattern of drug misuse is likely to be even six to twelve months hence.

As experts remind us, trends in the illicit drugs scene tend to be influenced much more by the supplies available than by preference or demand. For example, political changes affecting the stability of one supplying Eastern country can determine the pattern of drug abuse in distant places such as Britain and other European countries. The type of heroin being smuggled into the UK in recent years has been the deciding factor in the large-scale switch-over from injecting to smoking heroin, for instance.

In the past, cocaine was a scarce and expensive drug, the use of which tended to be confined to more affluent circles. Now, because of subtle changes in the pattern of supply, the drug is becoming cheaper and more plentiful. And city police are concerned about an increasing trend towards more widespread use among urban teenagers.

Some drugs listed below may seem so unusual or exotic that it is difficult to imagine them having any relevance to British youngsters. Yet a Birmingham teenager was able to give detailed information on the use of magic mushrooms which he had gleaned from unsupervised trips to the countryside. Another adolescent had tried the sadly misnamed 'angel dust' during a holiday abroad and found it a terrifying experience. In some cases, it has seemed wisest not to include certain details relating to drugs, where these might encourage someone to experiment.

In view of the recent widespread increase in the use of so-called body-building drugs in sports practice, some information on anabolic steroids is included in this chapter. Prolonged use of these drugs in high dosage may pose an even greater risk to health than the occasional use of some other drugs of abuse. Two drugs not included are tobacco and alcohol: they have been fully covered elsewhere.

GLUE-SNIFFING AND SOLVENT ABUSE
'Watch out for your own children,' warned the parents of a 17-year-old Surrey youth who died recently after inhaling the fumes from a bottle of thinner for typewriter correction fluid. The inquest was told that the solvent could have sensitized his heart muscle, so that rushing downstairs immediately after inhaling caused his heart to stop. It was pointed out that this crisis can occur with the very first attempt to experiment with solvents.

In a report in the *Medical Journal of Australia* in 1984, doctors reported the cases of two teenagers aged fifteen and sixteen who collapsed after inhaling fumes from a chemical used in fire extinguishers. One boy made a full recovery after intensive care involving cardiac massage and the use of life-saving medical equipment. The other boy died. Commenting on the tendency of certain chemicals to sensitize the heart muscle, the authors of this report said that dizziness should always be a warning to the 'sniffer' that a dangerous concentration in the bloodstream had been reached.

There was also a case of a 15-year-old boy who sniffed a litre of glue every day, which meant continuing to inhale for an incredible thirteen hours at a session. The story of this teenager's nightmarish enslavement was related in the House of Commons by Neville Trotter MP, who met him in the Newcastle clinic where he is now recovering. 'After one session I saw space-invaders who didn't look human . . . I felt frightened because they were coming at me and I couldn't move,' he told a *Daily Mail* reporter (24 January 1985).

'Sudden death syndrome' – the apparent cause of death in the first two cases mentioned – is thought to be caused by running or sudden vigorous exercise during intoxication. This is because 'most of the solvents and gases that are abused have the ability greatly to increase the sensitivity of the heart muscle to the hormone adrenaline', which is released into the bloodstream to facilitate action in a fright, fight or flight situation, Omar Sattaur explained in a *New Scientist* review (1 March 1984) of volatile substance abuse (VSA). This term is claimed to be a more accurate description of both glue-sniffing and solvent abuse.

Research conducted by Dr Joyce Watson of Glasgow University over the past ten years shows that most solvent-abusers are aged between thirteen and sixteen years, the age of greatest pressure to conform to 'peer group' behaviour patterns. The sniffer is twenty times more likely to be male than female. Sniffers have usually stopped so doing by the age of eighteen. Solvent abuse has always tended to be a group activity – a shared experience – but there are worrying signs that sniffing is increasingly becoming a solitary practice. Sniffing alone is extremely dangerous, because there is no help at hand if something goes wrong. However, it is not much safer in a group if everyone is equally intoxicated.

Current impressions that the practice of sniffing is in decline are neither as reassuring nor as realistic as one would hope, according to some observers. In some areas, it is claimed, youngsters are merely switching from solvent abuse to the considerably more pernicious bondage of heroin abuse. In other areas, the explanation for an apparent drop in the habit is that solvent abuse has become less visible because the sniffer is becoming more of a recluse.

This is the view of youth worker James Balding, who has been involved with the problem since 1981. With a group of volunteers and a £1,600 grant from the Queen's Jubilee Trust, he set up Solvent Abuse Helpline in July 1984.

'From our most recent work with glue-sniffers it has become apparent that many sniffers are going underground, in response to pressure from all kinds of sources including the media. By this I mean that they have taken to sniffing in remote hideaways – down storm drains, in squats or derelict buildings, at night in the park, in alleys and woodlands, and in the privacy of their own homes. And this makes our job of locating the sniffer and offering help far more difficult.'

About 50 people die each year in Britain as a result of sniffing. In 1983 it was responsibile for two per cent of all deaths among males aged from ten to nineteen. A survey of 282 deaths from 1971 to '83 by Dr H. R. Anderson and colleagues at St George's Hospital, London (*British Medical Journal*, 26 January 1985) found that 95 per cent of victims were male; 71 per cent were alone at the time of death; 51 per cent died from toxic effects; 21 per cent suffocated; 18 per cent inhaled vomit. Suffocation can occur in two ways. Occasionally, to get the maximum effect from the fumes, the user puts his head into a large plastic bag containing the solvent, and in an intoxicated state he may be unable to remove the bag quickly enough to restore a supply of oxygen to his lungs and prevent loss of consciousness. Another major risk of suffocation arises through the inhalation of vomit during intoxication (this can also happen with many other drugs, and with alcohol).

Solvent abuse has been known to involve, at various times, virtually every volatile substance used for domestic, cosmetic or industrial purposes. Solvent Abuse Helpline sets out the most commonly abused chemicals in four categories:

1. *Adhesives*: the impact adhesives are the best-known examples in this group as they contain toluene and acetone. The group includes cellulose paint-thinners and nail-polish remover.

2. *Dry-cleaning materials:* three main types of active ingredient found in many household and commercial products include trichloroethylene, trichlorethane (in typing correction fluid and other products) and carbon tetrachloride.

3. *Aerosols:* the active ingredients which produce the intoxicant effects are contained in the gases (fluorocarbons) which propel the contents for use. These include hair-sprays, deodorant sprays, paint and paint-remover sprays, household cleaner and polish sprays.

4. *Fuels:* these include lighter fuels and camping gas.

In a leaflet entitled *Solvent Abuse*, designed as a guideline for retailers, the British Adhesives and Sealants Association also includes in its list fire-extinguishers, solvent-based sealants and dyes, cold-start and anti-freeze preparations for motorists, and shoe and metal polish (particularly in aerosol form). It is very difficult to compile a complete list, for obvious reasons. (The fact that the current solvent-sniffing phase began with petrol-sniffing in rural areas of the United States in the early 1950s is worth bearing in mind.)

The methods most frequently used for solvent inhalation are to put some solvent in a small plastic bag (such as an empty crisp bag) and place the opening over the mouth (or mouth and nose), or to inhale the solvent from a saturated cloth pad. The two most dangerous methods are to encase the head in a large plastic bag (see above), or to squirt aerosol material into the back of the throat. This can have an icy impact causing temporary immobility of throat muscles (laryngeal spasm) and swelling of tissues, leading to suffocation.

Through inhalation of the volatile substance into the lungs, and thence to the bloodstream and brain, a mild intoxicant effect – similar to the effect of alcohol – is achieved within a few minutes. If inhalation continues the user may feel increasingly dizzy and confused. A pleasant feeling of euphoria may give way to frightening hallucinations. The depressant effect of the substance on the central nervous system can cause increasing drowsiness leading to unconsciousness. Vomiting may occur at any time with the risk of inhalation asphyxia. But if inhalation time has been brief, the effects will be greatly diminished within an hour.

The longer-term health hazards sometimes associated with solvent abuse were discussed in the government publication *Health Trends* (1982, Vol. 14) by Dr Dorothy Black, senior medical officer with the DHSS. 'Certain of the organic solvents have recognized specific organ-damaging effects . . . Benzene may give rise to anaemia and leukaemia; the lead in petrol may produce brain damage; dry-cleaning fluids containing trichlorethylene and trichlorethane may give rise to hepatic (liver) or renal (kidney) damage; butane is cardiotoxic (damaging to heart) and hexane affects peripheral nerves.'

General signs of solvent abuse may be difficult to recognize, unless glue has spilt on the skin or clothing, or the breath smells of chemicals, or there is evidence of intoxication. But once parents have discovered that a child is sniffing they are often able to recall changes in behaviour occurring over a period. These can include episodes of unsteadiness of gait; excessive giggling or irritability; loss of appetite, slurred speech, poor concentration and/or dilated pupils. Some of these symptoms may be seen only at weekends, when many teenagers prefer to concentrate their use of solvents.

Other physical symptoms often associated with persistent sniffing include redness and rash around the mouth and nose; excessive nasal secretion; watering of the eyes; chronic cough; and loss of appetite and weight.

For the majority of solvent-users, however, the outlook is encouraging. Most grow out of the habit in time with fewer long-term ill-effects than those caused by alcohol abuse. 'There is no firm evidence to date that glue-sniffing leads on directly to abuse of other substances, concluded consultant psychiatrist Dr I. Sourindrhin of Paisley, in a *British Medical Journal* report (12 January 1985). But special attention from doctors, social workers, youth workers and the community branch of the police force is needed for the lonely, chronic user who may also be using more dangerous substances.

Stressing the importance of health education, better re-creational facilities, and more help for vulnerable families in the prevention and treatment of solvent abuse, Dr Sourindrhin advised doctors on the best approach to children with this problem: 'Minimal, non-dramatic, non-alarmist intervention at an early stage, with the participation of parents, appears to be effective, and this is consistent with experience with other drugs, especially alcohol.' (This, incidentally, is the sort of attitude widely recommended for parents and other relatives, too, when coping with solvent or drug problems.)

New legislation designed to bring English law into line with the Scottish law prohibiting the sale of volatile solvents directly to children under sixteen is expected to come into force in 1985. While this should help considerably, a great many sources of supply will continue to remain outside the scope of legislation.

'We believe that solvent abuse itself isn't always a problem, but that it is a symptom of other problems. Consequently, our

approach is to help deal with the problems behind solvent abuse
– low self-image; problems at home, school or work and so on.
We do this by offering a confidential counselling service, initially via telephone backed up by personal visits if appropriate,'
explained James Balding of Solvent Abuse Helpline.

In its first three months Helpline received some 400 calls. Of
these 28 per cent were from parents; 50 per cent were from
professionals (workers with the police, social services, other
projects and the media); 22 per cent were from young people (of
whom three-quarters were male and one-quarter female). Help
was offered to the young people in a variety of ways, and
personal contact was made with 10 of the young people in
various parts of South London, Surrey and Kent. Parents in
contact with Helpline are invited to join a support/self-help
group.

In a survey of 50 young people (41 boys, 9 girls) who
contacted Helpline, the average age was found to be 16 years
and 5 months. Of the 50, 28 had made contact on the advice of
parents, 12 came of their own accord, 2 were referred by social
workers, 2 by foster parents, 2 by friends, 2 by other organizations (Parents Anonymous and Kick-it), and 1 each by a sister
and grandparent.

Some young people in the study used more than one substance. Of the 50, 35 gave information about the solvents used:
glue (24); gases (5); typing correction fluid (3); paint (2);
'anything' (2); petrol and sulphate (1 each). Two said they were
also using heroin and one was using cannabis as well as solvents.

While reasons for solvent abuse were not asked for, many
young people gave reasons – in some cases several. In a group of
20, 7 said they were influenced by friends; 6 cited unhappiness
as the reason; 3 parental pressure, 2 said they were bored, 2
attributed the problem to parental disharmony. One each cited
depression, seeking attention and having no friends as their
motivation for solvent abuse. In a further study of 30 young
people, 5 said they were occasional users, 13 were regular users,
and 12 were judged to have a chronic habit.

Many young people who have contacted Helpline are in no
doubt that the deciding factor in their initiation to solvent abuse
was boredom. 'Young people who are not doing well at school

feel they are wasting their time, and so they prefer to play truant and look for excitement elsewhere,' says James Balding. And because boredom is so widely recognized as a precipitating element in a great many forms of juvenile behavioural problems, this is an aspect badly in need of attention, especially at a time when employment prospects are poor for many.

In 1985, working with the International Youth Year organization and the National Youth Assembly in Lancaster, Solvent Abuse Helpline is co-operating in setting up other help groups round Britain, and in providing information about other local groups. (*See pages 55 and 57 for further information.*)

HEROIN

While other forms of chemical abuse continue to cause concern, the increasing level of heroin abuse among younger people is the single most serious problem of the 1980s.

Heroin is known medically as diamorphine, and to users by a variety of nicknames such as smack, stuff, skag, H, horse, junk, and so on. It belongs to the opiate drug family, and is classified as one of the powerful narcotic painkillers which are governed by the Controlled Drugs section of the 1971 Misuse of Drugs Act.

Heroin is listed under the Act among Class A drugs, which also include morphine, non-opiate drugs such as cocaine and LSD, and synthetic opiates and opiate-type drugs like pethidine, methadone (Physeptone), Omnopon, Palfium, Diconal and a number of others. (Class B drugs include amphetamines, codeine, cannabis, DF118 – a codeine-based analgesic – and as from 1 January 1985 barbiturates. Class C includes certain stimulant drugs.)

As the name suggests, the parent drug from which natural opiates are derived is opium, which comes from the dried juice of the opium (or Eastern) poppy. The medical development of opium as a painkiller is based on the power of certain of its constituents to depress the pain centre in the brain, and thus block out a person's capacity to feel pain for the time being. Because opiates can also induce deep sleep or narcosis, they are known as narcotics.

67

The history of opium was long established by the time Thomas De Quincey made its acquaintance nearly 200 years ago. 'It was not for the purpose of creating pleasure but of mitigating pain in the severest degree . . . a painful affection of the stomach that I first began to use opium as an article of daily diet,' he says in his *Confessions of an English Opium-Eater*.

De Quincey was born in 1785 and, like many of today's young people new to London, he found life lonely in his 'first mournful abode'. His only consolation, he says, was to gaze through the avenues off Oxford Street to the fields and woods which then 'pierced through the heart of Marylebone'.

The main active ingredient of opium is morphine. Heroin is a derivative of morphine and, in its pure state, is said to be between four and ten times as strong as morphine. Both morphine and heroin have a long medical history as powerful painkillers, in helping with post-operative pain, and in alleviating pain and anxiety in the terminal stages of cancer. Heroin also has the effect of depressing the respiratory control centre in the brain, which can be helpful in bringing a distressing cough under control in serious lung conditions. Clearly, this can be dangerous if the drug is used in large doses for so-called recreational purposes.

When powerful drugs such as heroin are used medically, great care is taken in the manufacture of the preparation, and in 'tailoring' the dosage to combine effective treatment with maximum safety. Even then, unwanted side-effects can occur, often because no two people can be guaranteed to react in the same way to an identical dose of the same medicine. Additional care is considered essential when prescribing drugs for children and younger adolescents, so that they receive the appropriate strength for their age and body-weight. In some cases, a potent drug might not be considered suitable for them at all.

Obviously, none of these precautions is possible when it comes to 'abusing' drugs obtained illicitly, which are obtained in powder form and are of unknown strength. Fatalities have been reported where the heroin supplied was of an unexpectedly high strength – more likely to happen in the case of an inexperienced 'pusher'. But the more likely risk is that the drug may be 'cut' or extended by the addition of some substance which is harmful in itself, and more dangerous if injected.

At street prices, an estimated £300 million worth of heroin is being smuggled into Britain each year at present. It is distributed in powder form – a brown powder mainly from Pakistan and white powder from China, according to customs authorities. Laboratory analysis of heroin seized recently by the Merseyside Drugs Squad showed the powder to be 30 per cent pure, which is considered a relatively high proportion. So it can be assumed that the average £5 'fold' or 'lucky bag' (depending on wherever you happen to 'score') contains at least 70 per cent of some other powder, which may be chalk or talcum, flour or another drug. Occasionally, something as lethal as strychnine has been added. Because of this risk, drug-users should be encouraged to report any unexpected or unusually bad reaction to a doctor, counsellor or street agency.

Heroin can be sniffed, swallowed, smoked or injected. Most younger users smoke the fumes produced when the powder is placed on a piece of tinfoil and heated. This is called 'chasing the dragon' – chasing the trails of smoke rising from the heated powder. Injecting the drug intravenously ('mainlining') is the fastest route to the target area in the brain; but it is by far the most dangerous method of drug abuse. Not only is it much easier to overdose in this way, it is virtually impossible to avoid painful and often dangerous side-effects such as blood poisoning, abscesses, damage to veins, and liver infection. Addicts who share needles also run a higher risk of contracting AIDS (acquired immune-deficiency syndrome).

If you consider the skill and aseptic precautions which are essential when an intravenous injection is given medically, the casual approach of the habitual 'mainliner' represents a horrific contrast. Very often, the greatest damage is not done by the drug itself but by the self-destructive injecting technique, observers say. Dirty hypodermic needles, often shared and used repeatedly, inevitably lead to localized tissue inflammation and the risk of liver damage, as does the injection of powder and water mixtures which are not surgically sterile.

No one is more acutely aware of these risks than addicts who have suffered such ill-effects and encountered scant sympathy when seeking treatment, through GPs or hospital out-patient departments, for a painful abscess. But this does not seem to lead to improved injection methods. And the 'solution' of some Philadelphia addicts – of self-medicating with illicitly-obtained antibiotics as a preventive measure – could result in worse trouble. According to Drs Scott and Sydria Schaffer in a report in the *Journal of the American Medical Association,* this practice could cause a build-up of resistance to antibiotics, making it much more difficult to treat any serious infection in the future. The authors warned family doctors against prescribing antibiotics too liberally without adequate cause, so that addicts could build up a stockpile either directly or with the aid of friends.

It is too early to say how prevalent this practice is among heroin addicts in the United States, or whether there is a risk of the idea catching on in Britain in the way that American drug-culture practices tend to do. On the face of it, compared with injecting heroin, swallowing antibiotics may seem a relatively harmless form of self-medication. Apart from the considerable danger of building up resistance to antibiotics so that this treatment may be useless against a future serious infection, it needs to be stressed that few antibiotics are effective against virus infections. And virus infection such as that which causes hepatitis is one of the biggest hazards of drug-injecting.

The day-to-day effects of heroin are associated with its ability to act as a sedative and block out physical pain and mental anxiety. It is this capacity, combined with the sense of detachment from everyday worries and the characteristic euphoria which can lead so easily to psychological dependence.

In reality, of course, heroin is not giving the user anything. On the contrary, it is taking away some of the power and sharpness of the central nervous system – the great natural powerhouse of neurological activity which is responsible for maintaining all our vital functions. So, as a result of this effect, heroin depresses the heart-rate and breathing mechanism. It slows down the cough reflex. It dilates the blood vessels, giving a false sense of warmth and well-being. It contracts certain eye muscles so that the pupils narrow down to 'pinpoint' dimensions. It slows down bowel activity, resulting in constipation.

The effect of heroin varies according to the amount used, the individual's level of tolerance, and various other factors.

Nausea and vomiting are a common problem for the beginner starting off with heroin. But these symptoms are also quite common with overdose (posing a threat to life through the risk of inhaling vomited matter), and they are very common withdrawal problems.

In most cases the general health of the heroin-user undergoes some insidious changes but these and simultaneous alterations in lifestyle may not be so clearly apparent to people who see the young person every day. Loss of appetite leading to malnutrition may go unnoticed in someone who usually has meals away from home, either at school or at work. Or it may be misinterpreted as an aspect of slimming and weight control. Lack of energy and tendency to mope about the house, with long spells in the bedroom, may not seem unnatural if the individual has been unemployed for some time. Symptoms such as loss of sex drive or cessation of menstrual periods are much less obvious pointers to heroin abuse.

Women are particularly vulnerable with regard to heroin abuse. Even where periods are irregular and sexual interest is lacking, pregnancy can occur. And while many heroin-using women have perfectly healthy babies, there is a risk that the baby of an addicted mother may be addicted and need life-saving withdrawal treatment. Because of this risk, doctors and midwives attending the mother need to know if she has a drug problem, so the baby can be kept under observation. (*See page 58 for further information.*)

The language associated with drug abuse in general and heroin abuse in particular is perhaps misleading in that it seldom represents precisely the individual's frequency of use or level of dependence. In fact, it is very difficult for anyone except an experienced professional to say for certain whether a young person smoking heroin has a physical or psychological dependence, or both. Compared with someone who has been injecting regularly over a long period, the young person could be described as having a 'light habit'. In such cases counselling has an important place in helping him not only to kick the habit altogether, but to resist any temptation to start injecting.

Terms such as 'addict' are also difficult to use precisely.

71

There is a case for not using such terms at all, on the basis that 'labelling' of any kind is damaging to the individual concerned and to his self-image. The term preferred by social workers in the field tends to be 'user', a politer word designed to reflect a more sympathetic, though not a permissive, attitude towards drug abuse.

Tolerance to a drug (or to alcohol) means that the body has adjusted to the continuing presence of an amount of the drug which could be toxic if taken by someone who has not developed tolerance. As increasing amounts of the drug are needed to obtain the desired effect, tolerance also increases. However, the reverse occurs when someone cuts down their drug use or stops altogether, authorities warn. Once tolerance has faded, it is very easy to overdose simply by taking what was previously a routine amount of the drug.

Psychological dependence can develop quite quickly even when heroin is smoked, and it is the most difficult dependence to conquer. This is the craving which drives the user back, after having survived the miseries of withdrawal. And it is the reason why many find it virtually impossible to beat the habit without supportive therapy.

Psychological dependence is seen as an emotional need to continue taking the drug, in the hope of achieving the relaxed, euphoric experience, freedom from worldly cares, which it promised initially. As the novice quickly discovers, this pleasant sort of 'high' is short-lived and, in an effort to repeat it, he has to increase his use of heroin in terms of quantity or frequency.

Physical dependence tends to vary according to the potency and frequency of heroin use. It can develop in weeks where the drug is being injected regularly; but it is not considered such a serious problem where moderate amounts are smoked rather than injected. Physical dependence is defined as a state where the drug has acquired a role in body chemistry, bringing about reversible biological changes through which a physical need is created. In other words, the body cannot function properly without a regular supply of the drug.

Evidence of physical dependence is seen in the painful and distressing withdrawal symptoms which occur when the drug is stopped. The level of physical dependence tends to be measured by the severity and duration of withdrawal symptoms. Though most people with a heroin-abuse problem are likely to suffer from some degree of both psychological and physical dependence, the compulsion to avert withdrawal symptoms suggests that physical dependence may play a bigger part in drug abuse among the very young than is generally accepted.

Withdrawal symptoms are said to begin 8–24 hours after the last dose of the drug. However, feelings of anxiety and physical weakness – of being 'strung out' – can start much earlier. Milder withdrawal experiences have been likened to a bad attack of 'flu with continuing aches and pains, the misery of a chesty cold, and perhaps a bout of diarrhoea as an aggravating discomfort. In such cases the worst phase usually is over in about 24 hours, although feelings of weakness may last for much longer, as the person involved struggles back towards a state of 'normality' (as most of us know it most of the time).

In addition to those symptoms already mentioned, more severe withdrawal can include persistent yawning, very severe cramps and muscle pains, loss of appetite, sleeplessness, vomiting, frequent diarrhoea and alternating shivering and sweating. The term 'cold turkey' is said to derive from the characteristic 'goose pimples' which tend to appear on the skin during a shivering episode. For someone who injects heroin regularly, withdrawal may take up to a week or more. In such cases it is always advisable to consult a doctor (who may be able to prescribe a short-term substitute drug such as methadone), before attempting to stop the drug. It always makes sense to ensure that a responsible person is available to help and give comfort during the withdrawal period.

Cutting down gradually as an alternative to sudden withdrawal is the method advocated by Dr Judith Morgan for younger drug-users seen at St Giles' Hospital, London, for whom a substitute drug would not be considered advisable. While the method calls for self-discipline and determination, it also gives the young person a sense of exercising control over his own actions.

According to the Blenheim Project, whose own 'Six Steps'

73

method of gradual reduction is described in *How to Stop: a do-it-yuorself guide to opiate withdrawal*, this method is recognized as the one most commonly used and among the most effective. 'Remember that most people who give up drugs do so of their own accord, usually in their own homes.' (*See page 58 for further information.*)

No one would try to pretend that giving up heroin is easy for anyone who has developed physical dependence. Even for young people who are thought to be only psychologically dependent, and therefore liable to have only mild withdrawal symptoms, the road back from regular heroin abuse is a difficult one to negotiate. The one essential prerequisite is the user's will to change his lifestyle. Without a personal commitment, nobody else can do much to help, as two of the most successful groups in the field testify: Families Anonymous (for parents and relatives) and Narcotics Anonymous (for drug-users themselves).

Statistics cannot begin to measure this problem, nor the sorrow it can bring to families, as Lord Elton observed in a House of Lords debate in January 1985 in which there were calls for tough legislation to punish traffickers in heroin and cocaine: 'Drug misuse sucks from its victims their health, wealth, their happiness and sometimes their very lives. It is not the dragon they are chasing – it is a vampire with fangs . . .'

Yet, while heroin abuse has never before been so widespread in Britain, there are some glimmers of light at the end of the tunnel, according to workers who see large numbers of drug-abusers. As Dr John Strang of Manchester has pointed out, today's average user is a far cry from the 'junkie' of fifteen to twenty years ago – those recklessly indiscriminate addicts characterized in Alan Bestic's chronicle of the 1960s drug scene, *Turn Me On Man* (Tandem, 1966).

Up to the mid-'seventies, when deaths from heroin abuse were very much higher than the current three per cent mortality rate for opiate abuse, fatalities tended to be due to causes associated with addicts' self-destructive lifestyle rather than directly to the drug itself. Casually overdosing was a common practice, which could occur very easily in a cultural environment where drinking alcohol, injecting heroin and 'popping pills' (amphetamines and barbiturates) by the fistful were considered the norm. This was the era of 'purple hearts' or 'blues', a combination of amphetamine and barbiturates which is no longer available.

One of the most reassuring findings of research into heroin abuse is that many addicts eventually stop of their own accord. A seven-year follow-up study of London heroin addicts reported by Edna Oppenheimer and colleagues (*British Medical Journal*, 15 September 1979) showed that over one-third of those known to be injecting heroin in 1968 had stopped using opiates seven years later. 'There is now considerable evidence that many opiate addicts stop using drugs after a period of addiction,' the authors say.

But what about those addicts – nearly two-thirds of the total – who were still using heroin at the end of the seven-year period? The researchers were unable to discover any clues at the beginning of the study which might suggest why one group might be more vulnerable – and therefore less well able to kick the heroin habit – than another. However, it was noted that those who stopped taking the drug were younger and had been using heroin for a shorter period at the start of the study than those who continued.

Not surprisingly, those who stopped taking heroin changed their lifestyles most noticeably during the seven-year follow-up. They were more likely to be in good health, have a job and a stable home address, and less likely to have contacts with drug-users or the law, than those who continued to use heroin. The authors quote from a 20-year study (*Archives of General Psychiatry*, 1973) by Vaillant, who argued that chronic addiction might be a substitute for stable human relationships. While the Oppenheimer study left some questions unanswered, it did show that those who continued to use heroin 'fared no better and no worse' as a group than when they were first interviewed seven years previously.

It has been estimated that without treatment about 40 per cent of regular heroin-users will have kicked the habit within 10 years. An American study by Winick showed that the average length of addiction among 7,234 users known to the Federal Bureau of Narcotics was just over 8.5 years; and that two-thirds of opiate addicts tended to 'mature out of' their addiction by the age of 35 years.

Commenting on these 1960s studies, Peter Laurie in *Drugs* (Penguin, 1971) points out that because of limited access to heroin at that time, few Americans were likely to be as heavily addicted as English addicts whose 'really massive habits' arose from the supply of pure heroin on prescription. Yet, he added, it was not unusual for users of up to one grain of heroin a day to give up the habit, and he knew of nine English users who had done just that. The winners who mature out of addiction in mid-life can count themselves lucky; but the pity is they have wasted the best years of their lives in such a way.

Young people tempted to experiment with heroin know little or nothing of the living nightmare which is the reality of addiction for the majority of those who fall under its spell. In a graphic account published in *The Guardian* (16 January 1985), Ann Kelley described her own experience when she provided a fortnight's respite for two addicted young people in an area devoid of suitable services of any kind.

'We went to bed but heard them shouting and crying in the garden,' Ann Kelley remembers. 'It was 2.30 am and Dan was halfway through the whisky supply . . . Sarah had a bad night of chilled sweating and nightmares. She cried as she told me that they had been injecting heroin, Sarah for two months, Dan for eight, and they smoked it before that. Dan first indulged in the habit when he was just sixteen . . . Hepatitis hadn't actually been diagnosed by anyone, but a nurse at a drug clinic told them they probably had it, as they had gone yellow and were sick for two weeks. They probably got it from a shared needle . . .

'They argue all day, loudly, about anything and everything . . . From the first day we treated them the way we had decided – they are children who have gone astray. They need a network of ordinary people who care about them; love and affection, a certain amount of discipline . . . They both took lots of pills, quarrelling over every administration . . . In the evening they fell apart emotionally and physically. At dinner Dan couldn't stop talking (about himself), and Sarah vomited without warning. Tears flowed: the veneer of normality is peeled away . . . Each day seems like a week. The constant emotion and drama surrounding them is exhausting – like having a new baby in the house . . .'

Fortunately, Ann Kelley's story did have a happy ending. A month after their visit, having separated and gone to live with close relatives, Dan and Sarah had stopped using heroin. Dan was attending daily meetings of Narcotics Anonymous, while living with his mother. Apart from one occasion when he yielded to temptation and suffered a severe attack of hepatitis, he had been completely drug-free for four weeks, and was neither drinking alcohol nor smoking cigarettes. (*See pages 56 and 58 for further information.*)

CANNABIS

According to ISDD, it is estimated that up to five million people in Britain have used cannabis at some time, and at least one million people use it in any given year. Used mainly as a relaxant and mild intoxicant, cannabis is recognized as the most widely used non-medical drug. Although it is strictly controlled under Class B of the Misuse of Drugs Act, distribution and usage are difficult to control in practice.

Cannabis has been at the centre of controversy since the 1960s because of the opposing attitudes of those who think it should be as freely available as alcohol, and those who insist that strict controls are essential on the basis that cannabis tends to lead to the use of 'hard' drugs such as heroin. One point on which there does seem to be consensus is that although proper scientific studies are desirable, they would be extremely difficult to carry out.

Cannabis is a product of the *Cannibas sativa* (Indian hemp), a distinctive bushy plant which grows easily in moderate climates. This is a factor which has encouraged its growth in some unlikely situations, such as window boxes, cabbage patches, well-kept suburban greenhouses and rural wastelands. Police found one of the richest hauls of recent years in a remote bog in the west of Ireland. Most cannabis imported into Britain comes from North Africa, Asia and the Middle East.

When fully grown the plant may reach from 5 to 15 feet in height. Its most important chemical ingredients are found in the resin which forms on the leaves of the plant. The commonest form of cannabis seen in Britain is hashish ('hash'), which consists of resin scraped from the plant and compressed into blocks. Herbal cannabis, which is known as marijuana in the United States, is a less potent preparation made from dried cannabis plants. The most potent variety – less common in Britain – is cannabis oil, which is a liquid resin extract.

The drug can be smoked, brewed as a drink or mixed with food; but the preferred method of use is to roll it into a cigarette, often combined with tobacco, as this allows more control over intake and gives faster results. Cigarettes are known by various names, including reefers, joints and sticks. Names commonly applied to herbal cannabis (marijuana) include grass, pot, weed, tea and so on. Marijuana is at least five times less potent than pure cannabis resin.

Effects on mood vary with the strength of the preparation when the smoke from a cigarette is inhaled. Reactions described include increased talkativeness, hilarity, intoxication, a feeling of relaxation, a heightened awareness of sound and colour. But the drug also has the effect of slowing down concentration, dulling mental function, and impairing co-ordination to an extent where it would be unsafe to drive a car. Unpleasant reactions tend to be increased with higher doses. According to ISDD information there is 'virtually no danger of fatal overdose'.

However, as Professor Peter Parish points out in *Medicines: a guide for everyone* (Penguin, 1979), very little is known about what happens to cannabis in the body: how it is distributed, broken down and finally excreted. It has been said that unlike alcohol, which is soluble in water and therefore quickly excreted via the kidneys, cannabis is fat-soluble and would therefore tend to accumulate in body fat. This could lead to a build-up in the body of THC. THC (delta-9-trans-tetrahydrocannabinol) is the most potent psycho-active ingredient of marijuana. Animal experiments indicate that THC alone can lead to the development of abnormal fat deposits in the brain and to a disruption of the brain's signalling system responsible for communication. Sometimes THC is offered for sale on its own, but experts warn that this is unlikely to be the genuine product.

While it is widely claimed that concern about cannabis use

has been exaggerated through lack of understanding among parents, members of the general public and law enforcement agents (until recently cannabis offences accounted for nearly 80 per cent of all drug offences in Britain, according to Release), there are some known risks. 'The effects of cannabis may cause special risks for people with existing lung, respiratory or heart disorders; and heavy use in persons with disturbed personalities can precipiate a temporary psychiatric disorder,' says an ISDD Drug Misuse Briefing paper.

A Colorado study by Drs Carol Blackard and Katherine Tennes, which was published in the *New England Journal of Medicine* in 1984, claimed to have established that cannabis does cross the placenta to enter the infant's circulation during the final three months of pregnancy. As maternal blood samples were tested only during this period (and cord blood samples were taken at delivery), the study could not show whether or not cannabis is also transmitted to the foetus, if the mother uses the drug regularly during the first six months of pregnancy. Nor could the authors say what effect cannabis might have on the unborn baby.

In another American report Dr Armand M. Nicholi Jnr. of Massachusetts General Hospital and Harvard Medical School (*World Health Forum*, Vol. 5, 1984), says that cannabis 'produces acute changes in the cardiovascular system that are similar to the effects of stress. By raising heart-rate and blood pressure, marijuana increases the workload of the heart and is therefore particularly dangerous in people with coronary atherosclerosis, cerebrovascular disease, or hypertension. Evidence continues to accumulate suggesting that long-term use impairs lung function . . . A strong statistical association exists between the use of marijuana and the use of more serious drugs.'

Dr Nicholi is convinced that apart from any risks attached to cannabis as a drug of abuse, it has decided effects on heart and blood pressure. He sees it as particularly dangerous where someone already has a tendency to high blood pressure, or where there may be a risk of a coronary attack or stroke, or where a person has any ailment affecting the lungs. He also quotes a recent comprehensive report on the drug which said that, while many important questions remained unanswered,

79

sufficient knowledge was now available to justify 'serious national concern'.

Drawing on a massive volume of 7,500 studies to 'counter the widespread myth that marijuana is a harmless drug', another American specialist argues that this misconception arose in the 1960s when only a weak grade of the drug with a low THC content was available. Dr Jason D. Baron, founder of the Drug Abuse Program of America, in *Kids and Drugs* (Perigee Books, 1983) points out that THC is only one of more than 420 chemicals which have been isolated from marijuana, which is a far more potent drug today than it was twenty years ago.

Heavy use of cannabis can affect not only the heart and lungs, but also the brain, liver, lymphatic glands (involving the body's immune system), reproductive system (reducing production of the male sex hormone, testosterone, and disturbing the female hormone balance). Regular heavy use has also been shown to predispose to some forms of cancer.

Those who insist that cannabis is basically a safe drug can be expected to counter these accusations with charges that conclusive proof of the drug's dangers is difficult to demonstrate. Even now the same claim could be made in favour of ordinary cigarettes, of course, although the case against them has been established beyond dispute. There certainly seems to be less room for complacency than the public has been led to believe.

Meanwhile, British medical circles report little evidence of serious concern about cannabis as a potentially dangerous drug of abuse. Indeed doctors writing to the *British Medical Journal* were quick to challenge a statement made in a report published on 7 April 1984 by psychiatrists at Northwick Park Hospital, Harrow and Shenley Hospital in Hertfordshire. Under the heading 'Psychosis after cannabis abuse' Dr Michael Carney and colleagues wrote: 'Psychosis after abuse of cannabis is well recognized, but we know of only one report from the United Kingdom. The lack of such reports has been used to support the case for legalization of cannabis.' They conclude from their own study that as cannabis abuse often precedes mental illness, it may have a causal role.

In a letter to the *British Medical Journal* in response to criticisms, Dr Carney and colleagues wrote: 'We innocently wonder if the absence of references to cannabis psychosis in British medical journals is due to the activities of those who want the use of cannabis legalized, and who assert that cannabis is harmless and therefore ill-effects cannot be attributed to it – ever. If so it is time that all the evidence comes to light and this assumption can be critically re-examined.'

A letter to the *British Medical Journal* from Dr M.G. Brook in Anguilla, West Indies, explained that temporary episodes of quite severe mental disturbance (usually lasting for under three weeks) were commonplace following a bout of heavy cannabis-smoking among previously healthy young people. 'Such events are a normal part of psychiatry in the Caribbean,' Dr Brook added, while suggesting that the average dose in Britain was probably much lighter and liable to produce fewer severe reactions. (*See pages 55 and 59 for further information.*)

COCAINE
Cocaine is a white powder obtained from the leaves of the South American coca plant. In Britain it is controlled under Class A of the Misuse of Drugs Act. Its principal medical use is as a local anaesthetic. For non-medical use, 'coke' has stimulant effects similar to those of amphetamine when the drug is sniffed up into the nostrils, which is the usual method of administration,

In the past cocaine was very costly and tended to be seen as a rich person's drug both in Britain and the United States, where it became fashionable in the late nineteenth century. It continued to be seen as a relatively harmless 'recreational drug' until quite recently. Only in 1977 did the US National Institute on Drug Abuse (NIDA) give the drug safety clearance for snorting in small doses; but after further investigation of the pharmacology of cocaine and the effects of abuse, the NIDA has revised its opinion.

Not only can cocaine kill, but it produces physical dependence in about half of all users, according to NIDA. This is in sharp contrast to the former belief that cocaine did not cause physical dependence and that it could lead only to mild psychological craving. A nine-year follow-up of 99 social users showed that half had gone from using from 1–4 grams a month to using

1–3 grams a week. And many had progressed from snorting to smoking and injecting the drug.

Another American report, published by a team from Stony Brook, New York in 1984, described a previously unrecognized hazard associated with snorting cocaine – subarachnoid haemorrhage (bleeding inside the brain). In two cases of women aged 24 and 29 years, haemorrhage had occurred within minutes of taking the cocaine. In both cases the sudden onset of symptoms such as severe headache, nausea and vomiting, momentary altering of consciousness, neck pains and visual disturbances pointed to the drug as the triggering factor when the diagnosis was confirmed by further investigation.

In the United States NIDA estimates that 22–24 million Americans have tried cocaine, and there is a continuing rise in the number of regular users. In Britain the problem has been growing in recent years, and there has been some reduction in the price being charged. Substantial increases in the amounts of the drug seized by customs officers, and in the number of people sent to prison for cocaine smuggling, are another indication of its increasing use. So concerned is the Home Office about the current escalation in cocaine smuggling that it plans to send its own investigative team to track down the major traffickers behind the problem in South America.

Meanwhile, in fashionable London society, cocaine use is 'rife among the upper classes', a television news programme has declared. 'Everyone is using it at parties. It's become so chic that it's absolutely normal. It makes you so lively and such fun,' a very pretty young woman explained. She said she was a friend of another pretty lady who had died after snorting a mixture of cocaine and heroin only a few months earlier.

Cocaine's physical effects include increased heart-rate and blood pressure, a rise in body temperature and metabolic rate, constriction of peripheral blood vessels, occasional nausea and vomiting. Regular sniffing can cause severe damage to the lining of the nose. Toxic effects include cold sweats, facial pallor, fainting, delirium, convulsions and respiratory failure.

'There is very little doubt that death can result as a direct consequence of the pharmacological action of cocaine,' says American specialist Dr Jason D. Baron. 'Given the horrible consequences of cocaine use, why do so many people begin and then continue to use this drug? My impression from treating adolescents who use cocaine is that a variety of situations occurs: many if not most have absolutely no idea of these side-effects; some are poly-drug-users who are looking for a new thrill; and many are relatively affluent kids who have become bored with marijuana and are introduced to the drug in a familiar social setting.'

It would be tragic if cocaine were to gain a similar foothold among Britain's adolescent population. It could happen if the drug were to become considerably cheaper and more plentiful than it is at present. It would be even more likely to happen if realistic health education were not available to help counteract the glamorous image of cocaine which tends to be projected at present.

BARBITURATES

Barbiturates belong to a group of drugs classified as hypnotics and sedatives (or hypnosedatives). This group of drugs also includes newer drugs other than barbiturates in the tranquillizer and sedative range. A drug with an hypnotic effect is designed to induce sleep. The sedative action is aimed at allaying severe anxiety, without causing sleepiness during the day. These are prescribed drugs which reach the street market only through the misuse of prescriptions or theft.

Until quite recently, barbiturates were the most widely used sleeping pills in Britain and many other countries. The fact that they were obtainable legitimately on a doctor's prescription made them seem an acceptable and relatively harmless medicine, compared with known addictive drugs like heroin which were not available in the same way. Yet it was from the family medicine cabinet or bedside-table drawer that many youngsters got their first experimental supplies of these drugs. The irony was that 'street-wise' teenagers often knew far more about the drugs than their parents for whom they were prescribed.

Barbiturates are extremely dangerous drugs when the prescribed dose is exceeded, and especially when combined with alcohol. A lethal dose need not be much more than double the prescribed dose in some cases. As drugs which depress the central nervous system and slow down vital functions such as breathing and heart-rate, barbiturates are potentiated by alcohol, which is also a central nervous system depressant. This means that the combined effect is considerably more powerful than that of the same amount of the drug or alcohol taken separately.

Throughout the 1960s and 1970s, barbiturates and alcohol featured prominently in the tragic deaths due to accidental overdose of many well-known entertainers. According to ISDD figures, 15,000 people were dependent on barbiturates in 1979. In their survey of a sample of 134 deaths recorded by coroners as being due to drug addiction, Dr A. Hamid Ghodse of St George's Hospital, London, and his colleagues at the Institute of Psychiatry found that over half these deaths were due to barbiturate overdose (*British Medical Journal*, 23–30 December 1978).

A similar pattern was being reported by voluntary agencies. In one year there were nine deaths among barbiturate addicts known at a day centre run by the Blenheim Project. The project's 1974 report, *People Adrift,* said that 'barbiturate misuse is more dangerous than any other addiction. Because people tend to get more intoxicated on barbiturates, there is a danger of barbiturate poisoning and fits occur if supplies are cut off.'

There were numerous reasons why barbiturate addiction posed difficult problems for users wishing to stop, and helping agencies, as a report by Tim Justin Robinson (*Community Care,* 7 August 1984) explained. There was the vicious circle whereby young newcomers to London could not find accommodation, took refuge in drugs, and then could not find regular hostel accommodation because of the drug habit. 'There are people who would not be on drugs if they had somewhere to live,' Blenheim Project social worker Frances Lowe said.

But according to Tim Justin Robinson, far from inspiring confidence and fellow-feeling, the user's behaviour too often gave rise to fear: 'Of all the drug addictions, barbiturate addiction is probably the nastiest. Addicts are violent if they are not unconscious, and the drugs are easy to obtain.' Moreover, the drug dependency clinics set up by the government in 1968 made no provision for barbiturate addicts, because clinic doctors were not allowed to prescribe the drug as part of a maintenance programme. (Since then, maintenance prescribing has virtually come to a standstill in the treatment of addiction in many areas; but for the addicted barbiturate-user, finding a safe way of stopping the drug remains a problem because of the serious risks associated with abrupt withdrawal.)

For many years, barbiturates served a useful purpose in medical treatment, and especially in the control of major epileptic attacks. In the days before minor tranquillizers such as the benzodiazepines (much safer drugs which include Librium and Valium) became available, barbiturates were much appreciated for their sedative effect in small doses.

As the dangers of barbiturate abuse came to be recognized, doctors were asked to limit their prescribing and, as a result, there was a dramatic reduction in the amount of the drug available on the street. It was only in January 1985, however, that barbiturates were finally added to the list of Controlled Drugs (in Class B). This means that while doctors can continue to prescribe these drugs, prescriptions must comply with certain regulations. This measure should make it even more difficult to obtain the drug illicitly. None the less, some supply sources will inevitably remain open while there is a demand. Early in 1985 a variety of barbiturates was available in London on a sale-or-exchange basis, with an average value of £1.00 sterling per tablet or capsule.

The most commonly misused brands of barbiturates include: Tuinal (orange/blue capsules); Seconal (orange capsule, also known as 'reds' or 'redbirds' on the black market); Nembutal (yellow capsule, also known as 'nemmies', 'yellows' and 'yellow jackets'); Amytal (white tablet); Sodium Amytal (blue capsule, also known as 'blue jays'); Soneryl (pink tablet). Fortunately, phenobarbitone preparations needed to control epilepsy are unlikely to appeal to misusers, as they are constructed chemically in such a way as to administer the drug very slowly on a 'sustained release' basis once it is within the body.

As drugs of abuse, barbiturates have effects similar to those of alcohol but with more marked personality disturbance, frequently leading to disturbed and violent behaviour. In producing drug dependence these drugs are much more dangerous than many others, not least because suddenly stopping without medical supervision can have fatal results.

Tolerance to barbiturates is especially dangerous because although you can become tolerant to the sedative or intoxicant effects you do not become tolerant to the lethal effects. While someone may need 'a larger and larger dose to make him sleep, it does not take a larger and larger dose to kill him,' says Professor Peter Parish, director of the Medicines Research Unit, Cardiff, and author of the book *Medicines: a guide for everyone*, quoted earlier.

Complications of barbiturate abuse include an increased risk of hypothermia due to the drug's effect in inhibiting the body's normal response to cold conditions; and an increased risk of bronchitis and pheumonia. Long-term use can lead to poor nutrition and general health, skin rashes and irritability. Symptoms of overdose can include signs of intoxication, difficulty in concentration, slurred speech, unsteady gait and blurred vision, emotional instability and depression.

At the other extreme, withdrawal symptoms can vary considerably according to the particular drug used and for how long and in what dosage it has been taken. Symptoms, Professor Parish explains, can include anxiety, restlessness, trembling, abdominal cramps, vomiting, general weakness, hallucinations, delirium, fits and even death.

Needless to say, medical help should be obtained immediately if anyone displays recognizable overdose or withdrawal symptoms associated with barbiturate use. It is also of vital importance that young people – and older users, too – should understand the dangers of these drugs, and of mixing barbiturates with other drugs and alcohol.

Considerable ignorance seems to exist among regular users about the relative evil properties of different drugs. One occasional user and dealer on the fringes of the London drug scene told me: 'I would never have anything to do with heroin – once you start using that you're hooked into real addiction. But barbiturates are something you might find on anyone's bedside table.'

While that is obviously an over-simplification, he could

quote instances where teenagers had found 'perfectly usable' supplies left over from a prescription which had been issued several years before.

'Very often the parents don't have any idea what the drugs are, because the label doesn't spell it out that this is a barbiturate or an amphetamine,' he continued. There was the case, for instance, where a policeman called on a woman to check up on a story told by a teenage neighbour found in possession of both barbiturates and amphetamines.

'It's quite impossible. We've never had anything like that in this house,' she retorted indignantly when told that the boy claimed to have found them in her bathroom cabinet. The fact was that they had been prescribed for her elderly father who had died two years earlier. This incident highlights yet another reason for not keeping left over medicines of any kind in the house. (*See page 56 for further information.*)

MINOR TRANQUILLIZERS

Minor tranquillizers are so called to distinguish them from the *major* variety, which are prescribed mainly in the treatment of severe forms of psychotic illness. Minor tranquillizers include benzodiazepines, the much safer anti-anxiety drugs which have largely replaced barbiturates from the mid-1960s onwards. Not only were they vastly safer than barbiturates, they were also found to be more effective because their action seemed to mimic a natural process in the chemistry of the central nervous system. Among the better-known brand names are Librium, Valium, Equanil and Ativan.

It was thought that the long-term use of these drugs did not lead to dependency problems, until doctors began to find that many patients were having distressing withdrawal symptoms if they stopped taking the drugs suddenly. One of the most recent reports on this subject followed the experiences of twelve patients, whose problems were studied by Dr Heather Ashton of the University of Newcastle-upon-Tyne (*British Medical Journal*, 14 April 1984).

All the patients had been taking only the prescribed dose of the drug. They were referred to Dr Ashton by their own GPs because of symptoms which they had experienced either while taking benzodiazepines or when they tried to reduce or stop taking the drug. All the patients had had a similar range of symptoms, and used the same sort of phrases to describe them at their first interview: 'I feel as though I were walking on cotton wool'; 'I feel as though there were a veil over my eyes'; 'I feel that I am going crazy'. On investigation Dr Ashton discovered that her patients were suffering from distressing symptoms affecting function throughout the body. Moreover, the symptoms could persist for many months.

Not everyone taking tranquillizers for a long period, or who stops taking them suddenly, is affected in the same way. Personality is believed to play an important part. 'Patients with passive and dependent personality characteristics are more liable to develop symptoms. By contrast, many patients can stop benzodiazepines after many years without any withdrawal symptoms,' wrote Dr P.J. Tyrer, consultant psychiatrist at Mapperley Hospital, Nottingham, in a review in the same issue of the *British Medical Journal*. In all cases, however, it is advised that in order to try to avoid or minimize withdrawal symptoms, the drug should never be stopped abruptly, or without the advice of the doctor who prescribed it. This usually involves following carefully a programme of gradual withdrawal, and calling for medical help with any troublesome symptoms.

In recent times the aspect of tranquillizer use which has attracted most public attention is the large volume of prescriptions issued and their cost to the National Health Service. A conservative estimate by Professor Malcolm Lader of the Maudsley Hospital, London, suggests that at least 100,000 people are dependent on these drugs in Britain, and the figure could in reality be nearer 250,000. The Standing Conference on Drug Abuse (SCODA) estimates that as many as 625,000 people have taken tranquillizers for over a seven-year period.

According to Michael Meacher MP in *Cold Comfort*, his report on alcohol, drugs and homelessness, the drugs bill for tranquillizers has grown enormously. 'Between 1980 and 1982, nearly a million new prescriptions were dispensed, and for the first nine months of 1983 (the most recent period for which figures are available), there were already 17.7 million prescriptions. The cost for this period alone is in the region of £27 million, already equal to total spending on tranquillizers in 1980. Total spending since 1980 exceeds £122 million.'

As is well known, twice as many women as men take tranquillizers. One reason given for this trend is that women tend to make more frequent visits to the doctor; and many of their complaints are of a type for which the doctor would consider tranquillizers helpful. Another explanation is that men far more readily find their way into pubs and, without thinking of it in that way, actually use alcohol as a regular tranquillizer. On the other hand, for a woman with severe anxiety problems, getting into the alcohol trap is not an acceptable substitute for tranquillizers.

It would without doubt be better for ourselves, and for Britain's exchequer, if many fewer tranquillizers were prescribed. This message is at last getting through to everyone, including doctors, which is all to the good except for one thing: there is a danger that people who really need this sort of support will not ask for it; and that if they eventually find the courage to ask, the doctor will try to talk them out of it, or issue a prescription for a very limited period. (There is evidence to show that this is happening at present.)

Does anyone have a good word to say for tranquillizers nowadays? Although doctors generally recognize their value where they are really needed, they tend to be much more wary about interpreting that need nowadays.

Dr Tyrer's summing-up in the *British Medical Journal* seems to put the matter in perspective: 'Finally, we should not assume that the long-term prescription of benzodiazepine and the consequent high risk of dependence are evils to be avoided at all costs. No permanent consequences of dependence on benzodiazepines have been described . . . Cigarette smoking probably represents the closest pharmacological cousin of benzodiazepine dependance and is far more dangerous – as is the addiction to alcohol that the patient may take up as an alternative.'

Like other drugs which act on the central nervous system, tranquillizers can be dangerous if taken with alcohol. This is because quite small amounts of alcohol can have a much more potent effect when combined with tranquillizers than if taken separately with an interval of several hours between them.

The need to keep tranquillizers out of the reach of children, and older youngsters who might be tempted to experiment, is also very important. In this case, too, there is always the risk that a teenager will be quicker than his parents to see the possibilities of any prescribed drug which is designed to act through the central nervous system. Even if the teenager does not use the drug personally, he may be able to exchange it for a smaller amount of a drug which he wishes to use. (*See page 58 for further information.*)

AMPHETAMINES AND OTHER STIMULANTS
Amphetamines are among the most potent members of a group of drugs classified as central nervous system stimulants, because of their effect in increasing brain activity and mental alertness. Hence the name 'speed' by which these drugs are known on the street market. Other names include uppers, bennies and benzies (from Benzedrine, once the leading drug in the group). The main stimulants are controlled under Class B of the Misuse of Drugs Act. Milder stimulants are in Class C.

Until about twenty years ago, amphetamines were widely prescribed for depression, and non-medical use tended to be confined to occasional self-treatment by people such as night-workers who found it difficult to stay awake. They came to be used heavily as a general stimulant for the first time in World War II, when supplies were given to troops on both sides of the conflict to combat fatigue. According to Release figures, over 70 million amphetamine tablets were issued to British troops at that time. And more than 225 million tablets were consumed by American soldiers in Vietnam between 1966 and 1969.

Today this group includes drugs such as Dexedrine (a yellow tablet) and Ritalin (a white tablet), both of which are prescribed to treat narcolepsy (sleeping sickness) and certain forms of hyperactivity in children. Durophet is used to treat severe obesity by reducing appetite through an effect on the control centre in the brain. Other less potent stimulants are prescribed for mental and physical fatigue, tiredness during convalescence and so on. Less potent anti-obesity drugs include Apisate, Ponderax and Tenuate Dospan.

All of these drugs carry the warning for the prescribing doctor that 'prolonged administration of central nervous stimulants should be avoided; such drugs may produce tolerance or psychic dependence'. The importance of taking such drugs only under medical supervision is underlined by the number of contra-indications and special precautions which doctors are advised to take into account when prescribing them. For example, various types of stimulants should not be taken by people suffering from depression, having a particular kind of treatment for depression, women who are pregnant, sufferers from heart disease or high blood pressure.

As drugs of abuse, amphetamines come second in popularity to cannabis, but a long way behind it, according to ISDD information, but more recently the emphasis on heroin has begun to modify this pattern. Most of the 'speed' available on the streets is illictly manufactured amphetamine sulphate powder, which is often adulterated by the addition of other powdered material (such as milk powder). The powder can be sniffed up the nose, swallowed or smoked mixed with tobacco. Mixed with water and injected, the powder can be dangerous – more so if something like milk powder has been used to dilute it. (Medical supplies of amphetamine prepared for injection come under Class A of the Misuse of Drugs Act, and there are heavier penalties for being found in possession of this form of the drug.)

In low doses used on a short-term basis, amphetamines 'arouse and activate the user much as the body's natural adrenaline does' says an ISDD briefing on the subject. 'Breathing and heart-rate speed up, the pupils widen, and appetite lessens. The user feels more energetic, confident and cheerful. Because of these effects there is a risk of psychological dependence.'

The effects of a single dose last between three and four hours and leave a feeling of tiredness, after which it can take the body a couple of days to recover fully. Feelings of anxiety and irritability are common. 'High doses, especially if frequently repeated over several days, can produce delirium, panic, hallucinations and feelings of persecution . . . Regular users of high doses are liable to develop delusions, hallucinations and feelings of paranoia.'

When amphetamines are used on a long-term basis, increasing doses have to be taken to maintain the desired effects. Because amphetamines only postpone the need to satisfy hunger and fatigue, an individual who stops using the drug is likely to feel extremely tired and depressed and ravenously hungry. Heavy use of the drug can damage the user's general health through inadequate food and sleep. It can also affect the heart and blood vessels, especially among those who already have high blood pressure, and athletes – if they exercise strenuously while using the drug.

As tends to be the case with most drugs, the effect of amphetamines can vary considerably depending on the individual's personality and body chemistry. Some people can build up a tolerance to much larger doses than others; while adverse effects such as severe depression and the overwhelming exhaustion of 'amphetamine crash' have been known to occur with relatively small doses.

Eileen was aged eighteen and worried about being overweight when someone offered her a supply of amphetamine tablets to help reduce her appetite. All seemed to be going well when the 'crash' came, suddenly and without warning.

'Apart from the fact that I didn't get the tablets from a doctor, everything seemed all right. They were of a well-known brand and I was sticking more or less to the recommended dose. I had never felt more lively or cheerful and I had begun to lose weight,' Eileen remembered. 'Then one evening I had just got off the bus on my way home and it suddenly hit me – this feeling of complete exhaustion that made me feel as if I couldn't walk another step. I just stood there, wanting to lie down in the middle of the pavement, but I managed to reach someone's garden wall where I sat for what seemed ages. Eventually, I got a lift the rest of the way home from a passing motorist, and I remember resting up in bed for days. I seemed to know instinctively that it had to be the drug, so I stopped taking it at once and I've never looked back in the five years since then.'

Stopping amphetamines is said not to result in physical withdrawal symptoms. But with increased understanding of the role played by brain chemistry in the cause and treatment of certain severe types of depression, it could be argued that the depression which is such a familiar characteristic of amphetamine withdrawal is just as likely to be a physical symptom as a manifestation of psychological dependence. In a recent review in *The Sunday Times* (6 January 1985), Dr Anthony Storr said that the fact that amphetamines can produce schizophrenic-type symptoms in some people is seen as further evidence that schizophrenia itself is due to a chemical imbalance within the brain.

Symptoms of overdose can occur with relatively small amounts of the drug if the user has not acquired enough tolerance to cope with the dosage involved. On the other hand, people who have been heavy users over a long period can often tolerate very large doses. In either case, symptoms of overdose can lead to a life-threatening emergency calling for medical attention and sometimes admission to hospital. It is therefore always wiser to call for help at any sign of an overdose.

Overdose symptoms frequently include chest pains, rapid pulse, high temperature, twitching and muscle spasms. Usually the affected person is conscious with his mind 'racing off' in all directions. More serious signs may include breathing difficulties, convulsions and loss of consciousness. In such cases, knowing how to apply a few basic rules of first aid could be a life-saver while awaiting help (see 'Overdose first aid' page 57).

Ignorance of well-recognized precautionary advice can considerably enhance the risk of an emergency associated with amphetamine misuse. A cardinal medical rule is that central nervous system stimulants should not be taken by someone who is using prescribed anti-depressants belonging to the MAOI (monoamine oxidase inhibitor) group, which have the effect of blocking the action of certain brain chemicals. MAOI brands in current medical use include Marplan, Marsilid, Nardil, Parnate and Parstelin. In some cases more frequently prescribed anti-depressants in the Tricyclic and Tetracyclic group of drugs carry a similar warning.

Amphetamines are sometimes combined in misuse with a variety of other drugs, including alcohol, barbiturates or heroin. Release warns: 'It is quite common for people to use amphetamine and barbiturates in an "up and down" cycle. If used together, amphetamine sometimes antagonizes the effects of barbiturates and makes it very easy to overdose.' It must be assumed that it is unsafe to mix any other substance with amphetamine, and that any unexpected symptoms associated with misuse of the drug may be due to adulteration of the street supply. (*See pages 56 and 59 for further information.*)

LSD

LSD is short for D-lysergic acid diethylamide. Also known as 'acid', the chemical is one of the most powerful drugs known. It is classed as an hallucinogen because of its ability to induce hallucinations and other dramatic mental changes. Though strictly controlled under the Misuse of Drugs Act, LSD supplies reaching the black market are often manufactured illicitly. It is claimed that very often substances being offered as LSD contain none of the chemical at all.

Estimates suggest that less than one per cent of the British population is likely to have had experience of LSD. By the late 1970s its use had diminished substantially from the peak recorded in the early 1970s, according to the Drug Indicators Project. But there were signs that LSD use had become more common again in the early 1980s.

LSD is available as a colourless liquid and as a white powder. The most common method of taking the drug is by swallowing it. It takes only a minute amount for an 'acid trip', and this may be taken in tablet or capsule form, on a sugar cube, or on a square or circle of absorbent paper. The latter method is popular for reasons of convenience. Paper 'tablets' are sold on the streets.

The 'trip' usually begins between 30 and 60 minutes after taking the drug, and the peak experience is reached after about two hours. The intensity of the trip depends on the amount of the drug used and the user's state of mind under normal circumstances. The effects of an average dose last for about twelve hours, usually having gone through several phases. There is no physical dependence, according to ISDD, and the fact that further doses are less effective for several days after a trip tends to discourage the frequent use of LSD.

Experiences described by LSD-users include intensified awareness of colour and sounds, a 'feeling of being outside one's body', mystical or ecstatic experiences and so on. Although there have been cases of injuries sustained (where, for example, a user jumped from a height under the impression that he could fly), it is claimed by observers in the field that such casualties are rare. Nevertheless, an occasional user describing a recent 'bad trip' stresses the importance of at least one completely sober person being in the vicinity when a trip is in progress.

In this case, the bad trip included nightmare hallucinations about being trapped in a dangerous situation, and struggling to escape. (On a previous occasion this man had had a very pleasant trip.) Other unpleasant effects which occur sometimes include depression, dizziness, disorientation and panic. The main hazards of long-term use are psychological rather than physical, according to ISDD, and may include severe anxiety or temporary 'psychotic reaction' which can usually be helped by reassurance from a friend.

Anyone with worrying physical or emotional symptoms should of course see a doctor. They may or may not be related to drug use, but it helps if the doctor is given the facts. The 'facts' may mean that the person concerned has also used other drugs, of course. Unlike those who favoured LSD in the past, it is claimed that the average modern user is involved in a 'poly-drug' culture, in which experience in the use of alcohol, 'speed' and barbiturates is not unusual. This is a potentially dangerous pattern of drug abuse which calls for much more than is available at present in health education relating to drug use.

While there have been many theories about the possible long-term damage caused by LSD, confirmation of these is still awaited in most cases. It is suggested that the drug may result in chromosome abnormalities in the foetus, if the mother is using the drug at the time of conception. (LSD is high on the list of substances which should never be taken during pregnancy, because of the risk to the baby.) Another theory – also unproven – is that LSD may be stored in the body's fat cells, and released back into the bloodstream in times of stress. (*See page 56 for further information.*)

MESCALINE

Mescaline (or peyote) is an alkaloid obtained from the peyote cactus, a small plant which grows in northern areas of Mexico. It has been used traditionally by Indians of Mexico and North America as an aid to relaxation and to enhancement of religious experience, the drug being thought to make possible a higher level of spiritual awareness.

The traditional way of using the drug is to dry out the crowns of the plant and eat them. When the drug was first produced synthetically it was thought that it might have medical value, but this hope was largely abandoned in the 1960s when mescaline became recognized as a drug of abuse with unpleasant and potentially harmful side-effects.

One of the most unpleasant effects of mescaline is a period of nausea and vomiting which may last for two hours or so, before the trip begins. Physiological effects usually include dilation of the pupils, increased heart-beat and a rise in blood pressure.

From the user's point of view, mescaline is a much less popular drug than LSD, with which it shares many qualities. Trip effects include illusions – often of a religious nature – and an enhanced appreciation of sound and colour. Since the effects of one dose may last up to 12 hours, there is an increased danger of accidents if the user is left alone without a responsible person being nearby.

Like LSD and many other drugs, mescaline use leads to tolerance, necessitating larger doses to achieve the desired effect. Harmful effects can include restlessness, anxiety, inability to concentrate, loss of appetite and loss of purpose. In some cases, frequent use may lead to psychiatric disorders.

'MAGIC' MUSHROOMS

Hallucinogenic mushrooms were known for thousands of years among the Central American Indians, but their use among young people in Britain is a quite recent development. And considering how well aware most people are of the need to distinguish between wild varieties of edible and poisonous mushrooms, it is not surprising that the idea of exploiting non-edible mushrooms in this way gives rise to anxiety among parents.

There are over 35,000 varieties of mushroom in the world, and the hallucinogenic drug psilocybin is found in about twenty varieties, according to Dr Jason D. Baron, the American authority on drug abuse. About a dozen of these varieties grow wild in the United Kingdom; the one most widely used is the Liberty Cap, which contains both psilocybin and psilocin, two potent chemicals with an effect similar to that of LSD. These drugs are subject to strict controls under the Misue of Drugs Act, but, while it is an offence to possess the drugs themselves, the mushrooms in their natural state are not affected by legislation.

'By far the greatest danger in Britain is the possibility of *not* picking one of the hallucinogenic mushrooms,' says ISDD, pointing to the great danger of picking members of the deadly *Amanita* species in error. Some of these cause death even in small amounts. This is a vital consideration, especially as it may take a considerable quantity of Liberty Caps – eaten fresh, brewed, fried or dried – for just one 'trip'. Surely the risk is too great?

The effects of hallucinogenic mushrooms were described in two *British Medical Journal* reports in May 1979 and February 1980. The first one, from Withington Hospital, Manchester, concerns the presumably rare case of a young man who suffered from a long-term mental disturbance after eating Liberty Cap mushrooms. The second report described the experiences of three teenagers in Aberdeen who were experiencing 'hallucinations of colours and speed of movement' with traffic moving 'frighteningly fast' after they had eaten mushrooms containing the hallucinogenic drugs. Their parents took them to a hospital casualty department, and the symptoms subsided after a stomach wash-out, without any lasting ill effects. As ISDD's *Drugline* said in a review, this case further underlines the danger of being near traffic while under the influence of these drugs.

'ANGEL DUST'
Phencyclidine (PCP) is a crystalline powder known by many names, the most popular and most inappropriate being 'angel dust'. Another of its names is 'animal tranquillizer', deriving from its use in the early 1960s as an anaesthetic for animals. 'Hog', 'killer weed' and 'peace pill' are others. Research into its possibilities as an anaesthetic and painkiller for humans was

discontinued in 1965, when it was found that one person out of every three undergoing tests awakened in a state of acute though temporary mental disorder.

Though PCP was first used as a street drug in San Francisco in 1967, it is only during the last ten years that its use has become widespread as a drug of abuse among teenagers in the United States. In a 1984 *World Health Forum* report, Dr Armand M. Nicholi Jnr. said that an estimated 8 million Americans have used the drug, and that 5½ million of these were aged 12–25 years. In 1978 over 200 deaths and 10,000 emergency visits were attributed to the drug in the United States. But according to Dr Jason D. Baron these figures are probably an under-estimation and in many cases PCP overdose tends to be mis-diagnosed as an acute psychiatric breakdown.

There are signs that the use of PCP is increasing among American teenagers. Authorities on the British drug scene say that little has been heard of it in the UK so far, and they hope that things will stay that way. But with the tendency for most American fashions to cross the Atlantic, the risk of a British PCP outbreak remains a possibility.

Of all drugs of abuse, PCP probably is the most dangerous and least predictable. It can be sniffed, smoked or swallowed. Depending on the amount of the drug used and the method of administration, it may act as a stimulant, depressant or halluci-nogenic. Low doses may produce paranoia and perceptual distortion (a sense of weightlessness, for instance), while high doses can cause convulsions and catalepsy (abnormal sleep), Dr Nicholi explains. In such cases, deaths can result from drown-ing or traffic accidents, without anyone realizing the role the drug has played.

One of the most hard-hitting campaigning attacks every mounted against PCP was the documentary film *Angel Death*, which was shown on American television in the autumn of 1979. The presenters of the case against the drug were Joanne Woodward and Paul Newman (whose own son was lost through an accidental overdose of other drugs).

Included in the film's case histories was a boy who had attacked passers-by with an ice-pick and kicked in store win-dows with his bare feet while under the influence of the drug.

98

There was also a girl who had watched her friend drown in a swimming pool: 'We were loaded with dust. Suddenly she started screaming for help saying she was drowning. "No, you're not drowning," I said. I got out of the pool and watched her. Even when she was at the bottom I said, "You swim under water real good." When I finally did dive in and get her, she was already dead.'

In a review of the film in *World Medicine*, Dr Michael O'Donnell listed some examples of extremely disordered behaviour resulting from PCP use. One man used a pair of pliers to extract all his teeth. A 16-year-old boy shot his best friend. Repeated use, even with low dosage, can lead to brain damage. Very high doses lead to respiratory failure and death unless intensive care is immediately available.

'The greatest danger of PCP is the small margin that exists between the dose that produces the high and the dangerous overdose. If angel dust does come to Britain, doctors and parents, and particularly teenagers, need to be forewarned of the horrors it brings with it,' concluded Dr O'Donnell.

DRUGS AND SPORT (ANABOLIC STEROIDS)
We have all grown up with the notion that there is no better way to ensure a healthy mind in a healthy body than physical recreation. And for most of us who possess the flair and the stamina for such activities, this does seem to be the case. It seems a shame that parents should ever have to worry that a keen interest in some sport may involve drug risks for their child, yet, according to the latest evidence, the risks are very real indeed once a friendly spirit of competitiveness is transformed into a compulsion to win at all costs.

When these costs involve taking dangerous drugs, with the aim of forcing the body to perform well beyond its natural capacity, then sooner or later the competitor will be into 'injury time' and wondering if the risk was worth while. In the past we have tended to associate these widely acknowledged hazards with top-class international athletes playing for high stakes and desperate to win laurels for their countries. We assumed that they understood enough about the risks of disqualification, if detected, and of premature death, to enable them to make a considered judgement.

But now a very different situation exists, in which those taking drugs to improve performance are teenagers, who have little or no knowledge of the substances they are being given and often only a remote chance of becoming top-class athletes, with or without drugs. The case of a boy who was given anabolic steroids at a well-known football club by a trainer who said they were 'special vitamins' to build him up was recalled at a Royal Society of Health meeting by Professor Arnold Beckett, a leading member of the International Olympic Committee's medical commission (*Doctor*, 29 November 1984).

In a hard-hitting condemnation of the current widespread use of anabolic steroids in sport, he said that sport could no longer be regarded as a contest between two equal individuals: 'Competition should be between competitors, not pharmacologists and physicians, and competitors should not be used as guinea-pigs.' Some drugs could cause aggression and impair judgement, he added. Thus, drugs could be hazardous to other competitors and spectators, as well as to the athletes themselves.

Professor Beckett denounced doctors and coaches who played a part in encouraging the emergence of 'pharmaceutical sport', especially among young people. He quoted the views of a doctor with an American football team, who said that to take drugs out of football would mean eliminating most established sides. It would also mean a reduction in the violence which made the sport so popular. 'The American public is paying good money to watch speed freaks try to kill each other.'

The principal drugs involved are synthetic anabolic steroids (steroids with a building-up effect), which are related chemically to the male hormone testosterone. The group includes prescription-only drugs such as Dianabol and Stromba (in tablet form) and Durabolin (which is injectable). These were developed medically to be given in small, controlled doses in the treatment of certain conditions: some forms of anaemia; certain wasting diseases; convalescence from severe illness; and osteoporosis (a condition in which there is thinning of the bone).

Doctors prescribing anabolic steroids in small doses for legitimate medical reasons are always aware of possible side-effects, and of important contra-indications to their use. They should not be given to pregnant women, for example, or to men suffering from cancer of the breast or prostate, even in small therapeutic doses. They should not be given to anyone with problems affecting the liver or kidneys. In some cases, heart disease or high blood pressure are contra-indications. Even in medical doses, they can cause fluid retention; and women taking these drugs may sometimes experience 'masculinizing' symptoms, such as deepening of the voice or facial hair growth.

It stands to reason, therefore, that the risks associated with the administration of large doses of anabolic steroids over a long period by inexperienced people are vastly increased. Describing them as potentially deadly compounds in a BBC Radio 4 *Checkpoint* programme (14 February 1985), Professor Ray Brooks of St Thomas's Hospital, London, explained that in large doses those given by mouth can cause serious liver damage; and some cases of liver cancer had been reported in athletes. Those given by injection could have very serious effects, particularly on women and children, he said. Because they are male hormones, they can cause some growth of beard, baldness and serious disturbance of the menstrual cycle. In both men and women the drugs could cause infertility, while in children they could also lead to stunting of growth.

'In the long term, all types of anabolic steroids have serious effects on the lipids [fats] in the blood, and there may be an increased liability to coronary artery disease and strokes,' advises Professor Brooks. 'These are very powerful hormonal agents, and I would strongly advise anybody who is contemplating taking them to avoid doing so.'

How much evidence is there that this dire warning is necessary – and that the golden lads and lassies of international sport tend not to 'make old bones'? Sadly, reports to this effect seem to be all too common. In a *Daily Mirror* report (14 December 1984), Peter Tory quoted from a study by Ukrainians in exile which said that 59 Russian Olympic champions, 24 of them gold-medallists, had died at an average age of 41 since 1952. The Americans had lost five gold-medallists at a similar age.

'The principal cause of death is abuse by drugs in pursuit of victory,' the Ukrainians report. Their list includes the names of boxers, fencers, weight-lifters, footballers, cyclists, runners, wrestlers and canoeists. Although initially suspicious that the figures might have been exaggerated as part of an anti-Soviet propaganda exercise, *Daily Mirror* experts concluded that this chronicle of tragedy seemed authentic. It certainly looks like a powerful piece of propaganda against the use of anabolic steroids in sport.

Meanwhile, in Britain, the argument being heard most frequently is that it is no use competing internationally unless you take 'dope' because all the other participants are using it. And for anyone with an interest in experimenting with anabolic steroids, finding a supplier is no problem, as *Sunday Times* journalist Anne Spackman has reported (10 February 1985) and as Roger Cook's teenage scouts discovered when they visited a gym in Berkshire to obtain supplies for the *Checkpoint* programme.

Knowing little about the drugs concerned, the two 17-year-olds decided to have a word with whatever weight-lifter seemed to have 'the biggest and best-looking physique'.

'He said what sort of gear did we want, and we knew nothing about it. He said to come back tomorrow and he would give a course for about four months, and it would cost £55. He didn't ask how old I was, who we were or anything. He said they would give us 1½ stone in body-weight in about two weeks. We would get stronger by 30 per cent, and our weight would go up by 30 per cent. He said the main side-effect would be acne-spots. He said he could get us some steroids that were about £340 for the course. He said there were a lot of people saving up to get these, and one bloke was going to sell his car so he could get them.'

Even 11-year-old children are known to have taken steroids, a Sports Council doctor told *The Sunday Times*. Very often the drugs are bought for them unwittingly by proud parents in the belief that they are being given a magical concoction of harmless vitamins and minerals designed to enhance growth and build up speed. Clearly, adults as well as young people need to understand that any substances capable of having such an effect are potentially harmful, and that large doses of vitamins and minerals taken over a long period can also cause damage.

Posing as an aerobics teacher and a keep-fit instructor, two reporters from the newspaper had no difficulty in obtaining supplies of three drugs, with dosage instructions at four times the medically recommended level. One of the dealers named in the article – a 24-year-old engineer – advised them: 'Don't take more than 2.5 milligrams a day to begin with. If you start getting any dizziness, sickness, pains in the abdomen or liver, then stop. Work up to 20 milligrams a day.'

Reports of mail-order drugs lists from Britain, France and the United States are an indication of the frightening extent of the traffic in anabolic steroids. These can be purchased over the counter in France, and legally imported into Britain at the time of writing, so long as they are claimed to be for personal use only. Trenbolone, which is being promoted in Britain as 'the best product available' to help increase muscle mass, is actually a veterinary hormone preparation. This is being used to speed up weight gain in cattle for the meat trade.

Ironically, the use of trenbolone as a hormone implant inserted behind the ear in cattle is a cause for concern in official health circles, because of the risk that some of it may reach the human meat consumer at *second* hand. The EEC Commission is considering a ban on trenbolone and another compound (zeranol), on which a number of branded products are based, as animal-growth accelerators.

Yet *Checkpoint* researchers were able to find trenbolone openly on sale for human use at a cost of '£15 for two syringes' early in 1985. And another contributor to the programme described an exchange overheard between a trader and a customer who asked for a supply of a branded prescription product. 'I can get you anything you want,' he said, 'but what we are taking at the moment is horse gear. We figure they would not give dodgy gear to million-dollar horses.'

The enormity of this practice will be appreciated if one considers all the vital differences which have to be taken into account when dosages of any drug are being tailored to suit a large animal like a horse, and much smaller beings such as humans, especially children.

103

As Dr David Cowan, one of the programme's experts, pointed out, all drugs misused with a view to speeding up performance in sporting events carry serious risks. Stimulants such as amphetamines may make it possible to compete harder, but at the expense of shutting off the body's defence mechanism which tells us when we need to slow down. The effect may be collapse and death. Both stimulants and narcotic analgesics (such as heroin) can reduce a person's ability to experience pain, so that an injury can be overlooked, sometimes leading to permanent impairment.

A great deal needs to be done officially to curb the use of anabolic steroids and prevent their use among vulnerable adolescents. It is the duty of the government to close the loophole which permits the free importation of drugs which are otherwise controlled, 'prescription-only' products. The introduction of tests during training is being considered by authoritative bodies such as the Sports Council and the British Olympic Association. The difficulty at present is that tests carried out close to an event cannot detect steroids use if – as usually happens – the athlete has stopped using the drug a few weeks earlier. Unfortunately, the longer-term ill-effects are less easily hidden.

5   A port in the storm

While both hospital and voluntary services can be expected to increase fairly substantially during 1985, thanks to funding from central government and bodies like the Mental Health Foundation, provision will continue to be scarce in most areas. So how do you set about finding help if you suddenly discover that your child is experimenting with drugs?

Parents' testimonies have revealed how difficult it can be to get help if you happen to live in a part of Britain where services are only just beginning to develop. Where someone of school age is involved, you can telephone the local education department and ask to be put in touch with a youth worker or the school welfare service. To find out about statutory and voluntary services, you can call the health or social services department, your Community Health Council or your Citizens' Advice Bureau. But, despite what many parents say about family doctors not being interested in drug-abuse problems, it is a good idea to start by taking the child along to see your own GP.

In many cases, of course, it can save time and agonizing uncertainty if you can find someone who can guide you at once in the direction of a self-help group within reach of your own neighbourhood. Fortunately, there is a national co-ordination body which provides information to the public as one of its main functions: the Standing Conference on Drug Abuse (SCODA) (*see page 147 for address*).

THE ADVISORY SERVICE: THE STANDING CONFERENCE
ON DRUG ABUSE

SCODA was set up in 1972 by a group of voluntary organizations, including Release, with the aim of improving

105

communication and avoiding overlapping and wastage of services. In the beginning SCODA represented about half-a-dozen projects, whereas its current list of 34 includes the names of many well-known agencies which have developed over the past decade.

So it is good news that SCODA started off 1985 in a more spacious central London office and with two additional staff members, thanks to government aid.

'We have the equivalent of five full-time staff. We are getting one extra staff member for England and Wales and increasing our Scottish staff from one to two,' explained Rebecca Hitchens, who is fieldworker for the area covered by the East Anglian, Oxford and Thames Regional Health Authorities. 'We work on a patch system which is more or less geographical. It is based on groupings of Regional Health Authorities in England and Wales, so that one person covers roughly a quarter of the whole area. We also have a small Scottish office in Glasgow.'

In addition to its work on behalf of member organizations (which include such well-known agencies as the Blenheim Project, City Roads, and the Hungerford Drug Project – see list on pages 147–65), SCODA is on call to help local voluntary groups and advise individuals: 'When a small local group is formed and decides that it wants to offer some kind of support, then we hope they will contact us at an early stage and that we can go and talk to them.'

Clearly, this sort of assistance can be very valuable where a new group needs practical guidance and wants to avoid overlapping with services already in the area.

'We are getting a lot more enquiries from individual parents who don't know how to get information about local services,' Mrs Hitchens said. 'Usually they know nothing about drugs and have only just discovered that their child has been experimenting. The first thing we do is to find out if there is a local parents' organization near them, and nowadays there often is one. We always advise them to contact any organization which is offering support to parents, because this may be the most positive step they can take at this stage. If there isn't a local group, it may be possible for them to start one. If they decide to do this, we will give them as much help as possible.

'We then explain what is available to the child in that particular area. While social services departments have a general responsibility for children and young people, they don't have a statutory duty to deal with drug abuse. Usually, there is a hospital facility of some kind serving each area, which needs a referral from a GP, social worker or probation officer – in most cases the person to see would be the family doctor. If there is a non-residential youth advisory or counselling service, such as Drugline in Birmingham or the Merseyside Drugs Council, we would tell them how to make contact. Unfortunately, these agencies are thinly spread throughout the country at present.'

It is understandable that in the first shock of discovery, parents' feelings may be ambivalent. They can range between overwhelming anxiety in the face of a mysterious malady; anger at being involved suddenly and unnecessarily in a seemingly impossible predicament; and profound shame at finding themselves in a situation they had never envisaged – being a family with a social problem. Where it is revealed that the problem has been a long-standing one, implying deceit and probably dishonesty over a considerable period, these feelings can be exacerbated.

'The first thing we often have to do when advising or counselling parents is to encourage them to stop thinking in terms of moral issues and bringing shame on the family, when a youngster is using drugs,' said Rebecca Hitchens. 'Sometimes they tend to concentrate on this aspect, which can be the least important. So we try to get them to see that what neighbours think isn't anything like as important as helping your child to get over this problem and return to health. Once they are members of a supportive parents' group, it becomes much easier to get things in the right perspective.'

Advising parents about what they can do to help themselves adjust to the situation may seem easier than trying to find some way of helping a specific child. In the case of young people under the age of 16 years, any treatment on offer is likely to involve working with the family, always assuming that the young person is willing to be helped.

'Parents of youngsters over sixteen are told that the young

person must seek help personally, because no one can do very much if he is unwilling to co-operate,' explained Jennifer Bleasedale, SCODA fieldworker for the North-Eastern area, which includes Bradford, Leicester, Sheffield and York. 'We are not in a position to advise as to the best type of help for a particular child. What we can do is tell them about the different approaches available locally. To help a younger child, parents may be offered counselling through the child guidance service or a voluntary agency. The GP may decide that it is advisable to refer the youngster for assessment at an adolescent unit, where he may be treated as an out-patient, or admitted for a period as a residential patient. If there is a long wait for a referral under the NHS, then it may be possible for him to have counselling or group therapy provided by a local voluntary agency.'

For people aged sixteen or over who wish help, the choices tend to be wider, although facilities are scarce. 'For someone with a long-standing problem, we might suggest that they apply for admission to one of the residential units run by voluntary organizations. There are three categories of these: those with a religious philosophy; Concept Houses; and general houses, many of which provide long-term accommodation.'

As the name suggests, 'Concept Houses' are based on a concept of behavioural therapy which was founded in the United States in the late 1950s by Chuck Dederich, founder of Synanon, the self-help programme for people with alcohol and drug addiction problems. 'One could say that the "concept" means addicts helping addicts to change or modify self-destructive behaviour which has led to their drug abuse,' states a report on Suffolk House (run by Turning Point). Residents take responsibility for themselves and their actions, and undertake routine tasks such as gardening, cooking, house-cleaning and minor maintenance work.

The therapeutic programme at Suffolk House has four phases: the first, for a minimum of one month, is a period of orientation; Phase 2 is a time for working out basic problems; Phase 3 is a stage where the emphasis is on social activities, voluntary work and planning for employment; in Phase 4 the resident goes to work while still living in the house. 'We are often criticized for our strict regime,' the report continues, 'and it is tempting to succumb and go for a soft option because our lives would be made easier. However, this type of community has a proven track record in that those who complete it find themselves well prepared to cope with the everyday stresses of modern life. We don't pretend to have all the answers and we recognize that this type of programme, like any other, is not suitable for all addicts.'

Concept Houses in Britain (staffed by professionals and recovered addicts) include Alpha House, Southampton; Ley Community, Oxford; Inward House, Lancaster; Suffolk House, Buckinghamshire; Phoenix Houses in London and Sheffield, and a new house is due to open in the Wirral (Merseyside) in 1985. All of these accommodate men and women, usually from the age of sixteen years upwards; and clients are usually required to have been drug-free for at least 24 hours before admission.

'In recent times the "concept" theory has changed quite a bit. Initially, it was based on the assumption that drug abuse tended to be associated with some underlying personality problems, and that treatment should be aimed at sorting these out,' Jennifer Bleasedale explained. 'Now, with increasing evidence that other factors may play a major role, adjustments are being made in the programme. The trend now is for "concept houses" to develop a more relaxed and less punitive approach, and residents are playing a bigger part in running them.'

General houses which provide residential rehabilitation include Alwin House, London; Bridge House, Bradford; Cranstoun Project, Esher, Surrey; Crescent House, London; Elizabeth House, London; Parole Release Scheme, London (for drug-dependent parolees); 235 Project, London (for ex-offenders and ex-addicts – drugs and alcohol). All except Cranstoun (Esher) take both men and women. Some do not take teenagers: Cranstoun Project (men, 20–32); Parole Release Scheme (21 and over); Elizabeth House (24–34).

Rehabilitation houses with a Christian philosophy vary in terms of the level of religious commitment expected from residents. They include Chatterton Hey, near Bury, Lancashire (men aged 21–40); Deliverance International, London (men under 40); Meta House, Bournemouth (women aged

15–35); Teen Challenge, Llanelli, Dyfed (men aged 18 and over); Life for the World Trust, Bristol (men aged 18–30); Pye Barn Trust, London (men aged 18–30); Yeldall Manor, Reading (men aged 18–31); Coke Hole Trust, Andover, Hants (men and women aged 16–30) Still Waters, Basildon, Essex (men and women aged 17–35); Iden Manor, Staplehurst, Kent (women aged 25–60).

Accommodation and a therapeutic programme for officially notified drug-users who are receiving drugs on medical prescription are provided by Roma House, London, which takes men and women from eighteen upwards. City Roads Crisis Intervention, London, provides short-stay detoxification for multiple drug-users in crisis (men and women aged 16–35).

'For those who don't seem to need or want residential treatment, we would recommend them to visit one of the "street agencies" which provide advice and counselling, and can help individuals work out what sort of further referral is likely to be most helpful for them, taking account of the options available in the area. Most street agencies have full-time paid staff who are counsellors and social workers, and most are funded officially.'

Examples of street agencies are the Lifeline Project Day Centre, Manchester; Birmingham Drugline; and the London services run by the Blenheim Project, Hungerford Drug Project, Community Drug Project, Release, Soho Project, Piccadilly Advice Centre, and many others. Clearly, there is an urgent need for services to develop throughout Britain, now that London is no longer the only centre with a large drug problem.

'We are also able to give callers information about NHS hospitals which have a drug dependency unit,' Ms Bleasedale continued. 'Most of these give withdrawing doses of methadone to adult patients who have difficulty in stopping opiates, and this process tends to take about three weeks. Not many consultants give maintenance doses of addictive drugs these days, unless there are exceptional circumstances. There is much more emphasis on counselling and social work support in the hospitals now; and the trend is towards a holistic rather than a purely medical approach. In other words treatment involves

110

looking at the whole person, his lifestyle and relationships, and not just the problem of his misuse of drugs.'

City Roads Crisis Intervention, which allows a one-month stay for detoxification under medical supervision for people using several different drugs simultaneously is one of Britain's best-known centres. One-third of those completing the programme go on to rehabilitation hostels, while others are referred to hospital out-patient clinics for further treatment. The sad news is that City Roads could only take about a quarter of the 1,200 people referred there in 1984. And, worse still, its future – assured only for 1985 – is threatened by cash shortage.

Like many others providing advisory services for people needing advice in this field, Jennifer Bleasedale has worked in several residential settings, including a well-known hospital adolescent unit and a voluntary residential centre. 'The Esher Association for the Prevention of Addiction (EAPA) was started in Esher, Surrey and now runs several projects in the South East. It is run on the therapeutic community concept pioneered by Maxwell Jones at the Henderson Hospital, Surrey. It has a degree of democracy built in, whereby residents who have been there for some time have a role in management. They participate in interviewing new staff and residents, and they are consulted about most of the decisions affecting them in the house.'

EAPA receives enquiries from all parts of Britain from young people wishing to join its 9–12-month programme, but can help only a small proportion of these. Self-referral is considered a very important qualification, as it implies strong motivation to beat the drug habit. Residents are accepted from the age of 16 if exceptionally mature for that age, but most clients are between 17 and 35 years. The house has four full-time staff and nine male residents, but a new unit will have a mixture of men and women.

'It's much better to have the sexes mixed, because it does away with the sort of masculine-competitive atmosphere that you tend to get when men are on their own in a group,' she explained. 'No drugs of any kind are used in EAPA houses. The therapeutic momentum is maintained very much by peer-group pressure, and the staff are there mostly to help things along. In time, residents progress to senior status, but they know there is the risk of demotion and loss of seniority rights if they slip back into using drugs. This doesn't happen very often. But it is sad that so many well-motivated applicants have to be turned away every week.'

Unfortunately, this is an everyday experience all over Britain at the time of writing.

THE DRUG DEPENDENCY CLINIC
Don't panic, don't over-react, don't condone or collude.

Do try to remember this advice if you discover that your child is experimenting with drugs. Even if the main drug of interest is an opiate such as heroin, don't let your imagination conjure up a nightmare scenario recalled from some lurid account of heroin addiction.

While it is true that all drugs, and particularly heroin, are potentially dangerous, it is unlikely that your child is in immediate physical danger. Though three out of every hundred opiate addicts eventually die of their addiction – usually combined with other factors like simultaneous alcohol abuse, mixing drugs and malnutrition – there is a very good chance that your child will overcome the habit long before he becomes physically addicted to the drug.

This is the view expressed by doctors, social workers and many experienced parent-group members to whom I have spoken. Of course, it is asking a lot to say, 'Don't panic,' when you are shocked and distressed. We all know that feeling of alarm you get when a child has a symptom which could mean something more than a transient childhood ailment. 'Keep calm and don't communicate your anxiety to the child,' is the advice, and you do try. But inevitably some of your concern spills over, and perhaps this is one of the child's ways of gauging the extent of your affection and his own value in the scheme of things.

Parents with children on drugs may already be over-anxious about a youngster's health by the time the true nature of his problem is known. Symptoms such as poor appetite, constipation, a chronic cough and a stuffy nose can mislead parents into thinking that they have a delicate child who needs special care, according to Dr Judith Morgan, who runs a drug dependency clinic for out-patients at St Giles' Hospital, London, and an in-patient unit at Bexley Hospital, Kent. (These are two programmes sharing in recent government grants.)

Dr Morgan's referrals come through GPs, social workers and probation officers. Her hospital residential unit has twenty beds for patients aged from sixteen upwards, with a preponderence ranging from twenty to the late twenties in age. Referrals of 16-year-olds are not very common at present; there have been no referrals of youngsters under sixteen and the unit does not have facilities for them. One reason for this may be the widely held view that it is usually more appropriate for younger drug-users to live at home and receive help within the context of a family relationship.

'As a rule, adolescents are not very motivated to stop the drug,' Dr Morgan explains. 'We assess all applicants for admission to the unit on an out-patient basis, and it may need several interviews to assess the situation adequately, and in particular the motivation to come off drugs. In the case of youngsters, we find very often that they are very ambivalent about stopping, and that it may be the parents who are putting on pressure for them to agree to treatment. If youngsters do not really wish to stop taking drugs, it may be better for them to receive counselling about regulating their abuse. Admission too early may be a waste of everyone's time and money. Also, the admission of unmotivated people to a drugs unit can disturb other patients' treatment.'

By their nature, teenagers are not disposed to be co-operative. And some bring to adolescence additional vulnerability stemming from a history of childhood emotional problems. 'Drug dependence is a problem of adolescence,' claims Dr Morgan. 'It is part of the conflict between the natural desire to assert one's individuality and the fear of independence and of having to take responsibility for yourself. People who have problems in coming to terms with this conflict are much more likely to become dependent on drugs. Drug abuse is a way of opting out of responsibility and out of growing up, and it is a means of rejecting authority.'

What sort of signs would lead a parent to suspect that a child

113

was misusing drugs? 'The chief symptoms are behavioural symptoms, rather than physical clues such as 'pinpoint' pupils which we have been taught to associate with opiates,' advises Dr Morgan. 'The more obvious signs are changes in behaviour so that the child is more withdrawn and secretive. Variations in mood are common: at one time the child is very lively, at another he appears very depressed. There may be physical symptoms like occasional nausea and constipation. The child may sometimes appear intoxicated and actually have pinpoint pupils. But one of the most telling signs is that he gets through a lot of money with very little to show for it.'

Another pattern of behaviour which parents have remarked on is a general apathy with regard to any discussion of future plans, and a reluctance to leave the shelter of the family home. This is very much in accord with Dr Morgan's observations about fear of independence, in contrast to the desire of many youngsters to branch out on their own as soon as possible.

Once confronted with the knowledge that a child is using drugs, what can parents do? Dr Morgan considers that unless the child wants help, it is very difficult to give it. Parents' attitudes are very important in other ways, however. 'If parents were in the habit of treating the youngster as ill before they knew that his problems were due to drugs, then they may need help perhaps by counselling or a self-help group to come to terms with the situation, and be realistic in helping the youngster.

'We always look at the situation as a whole within the family, because unless you look at the family as a unit you are not going to get anywhere. Very often there are precipitating problems within the family, and the youngster may be using a number of different drugs without being addicted. When you work with parents and youngsters separately, or occasionally together in family therapy, you often find that there are family problems either between the parents or between the parents and the youngster, or involving other children. A pattern which we find very frequently is that of a vulnerable youngster who had emotional problems to start with, and who finds that for him, drugs are a form of self-medication.'

It is important for parents to avoid a situation where they

114

appear to be condoning behaviour which would be unacceptable in the ordinary way, Dr Morgan insists. If the young
person is stealing from the home, or bringing home companions
whose behaviour would not otherwise be considered acceptable
parents should do something to put a stop to it. Through
membership of a parents' support group, they can draw on the
strength and wisdom of those with more experience to help
them deal with the problem.

Very often the only option available is to report your child's
activities to the police, some parents claim. Others argue that
locking youngsters up does not really help, and may in fact
increase their risk of becoming involved in a criminal culture; it
has even been known for juveniles to gain access to drugs in
detention. But in the absence of the kind of services which they
see as being necessary, many parents see imprisonment as the
only hope of cutting youngsters off from their source of supply,
and, they would hope, keeping them 'clean' long enough for the
craving to subside.

Dr Morgan tends to agree with this view: 'I think that
something like going to prison can bring a youngster up with a
jolt. Coming before a court, or being detoxified in prison or
while on remand, can provide youngsters with something like a
"space" in which they have time to think about themselves and
where they are going. However, it takes a while before many of
them are ready to face up to this sort of self-examination,
because they find that taking heroin is pleasant and they haven't
yet learnt about its unpleasant side, which is mainly to do with
maintaining financial resources to support the habit.'

Many professionals working in this field hold the view that
physical dependence is rare among younger heroin-users: because they smoke the drug instead of injecting it; because many
are occasional rather than regular users; because many have
been taking the drug for a relatively short time. It is very
difficult for the average person to distinguish between physical
dependence (needing the drug to prevent pain) and psychological dependence (craving the drug for the sense of relaxation it
can bring). But can parents tell for sure that their youngsters are
physically addicted, even when they have been on drugs for two
or more years?

Professionals say they cannot, because physical dependence is slow to develop, which must be seen as one ray of hope on a gloomy horizon. 'I have seen a great many youngsters whose parents say they suffer very severe physical withdrawal symptoms and found that they were able to give up drugs quite easily, in fact,' Dr Morgan says. 'It is not a question of parents consciously exaggerating the symptoms, but more a matter of them seeming so much worse to the parent who has got into the habit of seeing the youngster as being ill anyway. But you can have a very strong psychological component, and we will quite often admit as an in-patient someone who has a psychological problem but not bad physical dependence. Incidentally, we should tell parents that withdrawal from heroin is not life-threatening, and reassure them that the worst part is psychological craving.'

Attendances at the out-patients clinic at St Giles' Hospital vary a lot, according to Dr Morgan. While some patients keep regular appointments, others visit the clinic only when some crisis occurs in relation to their drug-taking. While the patient's own GP is kept informed about his patient, a GP's letter is not essential for a referral, which can be made through a social worker or probation officer. (This sort of crisis does not include emergencies such as overdose, whether suspected or known to have been taken: in such cases the patient should be taken without delay to a hospital casualty or accident and emergency department.)

Adult patients who would otherwise have difficulty in coming off opiates are given methadone in withdrawing doses, but teenagers are not given drugs for this purpose. 'I am very wary about prescribing drugs for youngsters at all. I believe drugs can cause a lot of damage where the personality is not yet properly formed,' Dr Morgan explains.

'With youngsters, I would encourage them to cut down their own use of whatever drug they are using outside the hospital, and if they are well motivated they will do this. I find that this is a better way to wean them off. If you were to prescribe a drug it could possibly make matters worse, whereas [young people] feel they have achieved more if they are in charge themselves. The only thing I will prescribe sometimes is treatment to help with withdrawal symptoms like diarrhoea. But parents often find it disturbing that, although the youngster is being treated, he is still using drugs which he obtained illegally. Yet another reason why we believe it works is because it helps to get the youngsters over anti-authority feelings.'

On the currently controversial question of maintenance doses of a drug to which an individual is addicted, some specialists say they should not be used under any circumstances, while others take a more flexible view.

'There are arguments for and against this practice,' Dr Morgan concludes. 'I would never give a maintenance prescription to a youngster. If it is to be used at all, maintenance should be limited to patients one has known for quite some times, and who can function quite normally on this kind of support. But it is a very difficult decision.'

While medical specialists tend to differ in their policies regarding the prescription of maintenance doses of an addictive drug to carefully selected patients, many use maintenance occasionally. Others, however, are adamant that this policy can do more harm than good. Among these is Dr John Strang of Prestwich Hospital, Manchester.

'On the question of prescribing heroin on demand to people with an addiction problem, I cannot overstate my belief that this is a mistaken approach – that we are confirming them in their drug-using status instead of working against it,' he told a recent conference. 'There would be vastly greater numbers who would be cocooned from stress by this method, making drug abuse comfortable for them.

'If we were to apply the concept of maintenance prescribing to alcohol problems, it would be easy to visualize the numbers who would gladly queue up for their daily dose, and agree to try not to be a nuisance and get off our backs. This is just a way of sweeping the problem under the carpet.'

Another specialist who believes that the physical symptoms of withdrawal from heroin often tend to be exaggerated is Dr Martin Mitcheson, consultant in the drug dependency unit at University College Hospital, London. Writing in *Mims Magazine* recently, he said: 'It should be emphasized that physiological withdrawal of opiates is not particularly difficult, whereas the patient's capacity to cope with the psychological distress is overwhelmingly important.' Dr Mitcheson was giving advice to family doctors, of course, and it is envisaged that GPs will play a much greater part in treating addiction in future.

Withdrawal from an opiate drug for the patient with a fairly light habit (which would include the majority of teenage heroin-smokers, several observers have noted), requires no special medication, according to Dr Mitcheson. What is needed are supportive measures: reassurance and encouragement, pleasant non-alcoholic drinks, aspirin and hot-water bottles to help relieve physical discomfort, massage to painful muscles and a change of clothing.

Going it alone with 'cold turkey' is obviously not a pleasant experience, but it can be got through without medical help so long as there is an attentive parent or responsible friend to give comfort, and recognize the need to call a doctor if necessary.

FAMILIES ANONYMOUS
Without the understanding and support provided by counsellors, therapists and experienced self-help groups, families of drug-abusers usually find it very difficult to react in a way which is going to help in long-term rehabilitation. An organization which has proved most helpful in this respect is Families Anonymous, which now has 28 local groups throughout the United Kingdom and Ireland (including four groups in Dublin and one in Glasgow).

Families Anonymous (FA) is a fellowship of relatives and friends of people involved in the misuse of drugs, or young people with related problems, such as runaways, delinquents, under-achievers at school. It provides a self-help programme based on the Twelve Steps and Twelve Traditions which form a spiritual basis for group study, first formulated by Alcoholics Anonymous, and used by Al-Anon (for relatives of Alcoholics) and Narcotics Anonymous. Families Anonymous is not a religious programme – each member's understanding of a 'Higher Power' is seen as being a private, personal choice. Only first names are used. Membership is free.

'People must not expect miracles when they join FA, but we do have some marvellous results,' says London member Denny. 'We do a lot of liaison work with hospitals, and more and more hospitals are referring young people to us for help and support.' University College Hospital, London, is one of the referring hospitals. 'There are no simple answers, but FA provides a forum where families can share their anxieties and gain confidence and courage to adopt an honest and consistent approach towards the patient which will help him in his good intentions to live without drugs,' wrote University College Hospital psychiatrist Dr Jean Garner in the leaflet *The Professional Looks at FA*.

Another tesitmony comes from Dennis Yandoli, senior social worker in the drug dependency clinic at St Mary's Hospital, London: 'We have seen FA work and have applied the principles and programme to our treatment of drug-users and their families. FA has made it possible to offer a real alternative to families who have struggled with drug abuse.'

'It is truly inspiring to see, as I have done, people who arrive at their first [FA] meeting shaken, depressed and barely able to speak, gaining in strength and self-confidence from the programme as the weeks go by, until in their turn they are able to help and comfort those who follow in their footsteps,' wrote Surrey GP Dr Ian Fergusson.

The family of an addict suffers from a variety of powerful and painful emotions, including fear, guilt, anger and a dreadful feeling of helplessness. They need support so that they can learn that the addict has an illness and that the family is not to blame for it, and that they can best be of help to the addict by allowing him or her to take responsibility for the consequences of disturbed behaviour. I believe that regular attendance at meetings of Families Anonymous is unequalled as a way of achieving this understanding and so returning to normality,' said Dr Philip Golding, consultant in drug addiction and alcoholism in Bristol.

Another testimonial came from family therapist Dr Evelyn Hickey of the Charter Clinic's chemical dependency unit in London: 'Families Anonymous has revolutionized the treatment of addictive disease. I know of no greater source of help for the grief, bewilderment and despair that affects all those whose close relative has become involved in drug abuse.'

When troubled relatives turn to their pastor for advice,

finding a way to help can pose problems for a clergyman, as Dagenham RC parish priest Father Richard La Madeleine explained: 'I was very ignorant about even the physical dimension of drug use and abuse. I was frightened by the complexity of the problem, confused by the deception I had experienced from the drug addict, and I felt extremely helpless in giving practical advice to the family. Relief in dealing with this area of ministry and confidence in being able to do something effective came with my discovery of Families Anonymous.'

Families Anonymous's programme includes a daunting list of 'don'ts' for relatives, presented as an 'Open Letter to my Family' from an addict: 'I am a drug-abuser. I need help. Don't solve my problems for me. This only makes me lose respect for you – and for myself. Don't lecture, moralize, scold, blame, or argue whether I'm stoned or sober. It may make you feel better, but it only makes the situation worse. Don't accept my promises. The nature of my illness prevents my keeping them, even though I mean them at the time. Promises are only my way of postponing pain. And don't keep switching agreements; if an agreement is made, stick to it. Don't lose your temper with me. It will destroy you and any possibility of helping me.

'Don't let your anxiety for me make you do what I should do for myself. Don't believe everything that I tell you. Often I don't even know the truth – let alone tell it. Don't cover up or try to spare me the consequences of my using. It may reduce the crisis, but it will make my illness worse. Above all, don't run away from reality as I do. Drug dependence, my illness, gets worse as my using continues . . . I need help – from a doctor, a psychologist, a counsellor, from some people in a self-help programme who have recovered from a drug problem themselves – and from a Power greater than myself.'

Irrespective of religious commitment in denominational terms, the spiritual element in the programmes of Families Anonymous, Narcotics Anonymous and their forerunner (Alcoholics Anonymous) is a very great source of strength, according to Sue, who is the mother of a recovered heroin addict: 'I am convinced that the only way to real recovery is through participation in the NA and FA programme by the addict and the relatives respectively, because we are dealing with an illness of the body, mind and spirit. It was the only method that worked with my son, and I know my own life has completely changed through membership of FA over the past two years.'

The philosophy of these programmes certainly is a very persuasive one. The person in trouble is not being asked to do the impossible – to strive for unattainable success or climb high mountain peaks, metaphorically speaking. He or she is being offered success in reaching a goal which is attainable for most people, though it may be difficult for someone with an addiction, which is to face up to life as it comes, 'one day at a time'. And always present is the friendly support of the programme's membership, and the sense of drawing strength from that 'greater Power' whose help is invoked in the prayer at each meeting.

But surely there must be more to it than that – some secret formula – to win the Families Anonymous programme such wide acclaim? Sue explains that a common misapprehension among newcomers to Families Anonymous is the expectation that they will be told what to do: 'But this doesn't happen at all. What does happen is that you sit there and listen to other relatives' experiences and learn from them. And the first thing you have to realize is that there is nothing you can do to help the person with the problem. But you can do something about yourself, which means learning how to change your own attitudes and your present way of dealing with the situation. For most parents this is something they have never thought of before.

'What happens in practice is that once you change your method of dealing with the addict, he is forced to change. For example, you have to change your thinking with regard to supplying him with money, because you're only helping him to go on taking heroin. It's easy to give in when he asks for money, because he is your child and he looks so ill, and for a host of other reasons, but what you are doing is supporting a habit that is ruining his life and could kill him eventually. The minute you stop supporting the habit you tell him, "I am changing because it is killing me and I must help myself."

'When this happens, the addict has to make a choice, and in

121

FA we have seen over and over again how positive this can be. Very often it can be a slow process, but there are occasions when results are more rapid because the addict has reached rock bottom and he says he wants help from a treatment centre or some other source. When this stage is reached we do everything possible to get the most suitable help that there is available. At no time will the addict be involved with the FA programme, but he will be encouraged to join Narcotics Anonymous. From the start it must be made clear to him that FA is your programme – you are going to the meetings to help *yourself.*'

On a simplistic basis, caring for an addict could be likened to looking after a child with measles, Sue explained. If it is a bad attack you know that complications can arise and you become over-anxious. If you have not previously acquired an immunity you know there is a good chance you are going to catch the illness yourself.

'Obviously, you're not going to catch the addiction; but what you do catch are the mental stresses that go with it, so that you are constantly over-reacting to a very worrying illness situation. The difference, when you get better, is that the addict stops reacting to your disturbed feelings, and he begins to catch some of your growing normality. By helping yourself in this way you can improve all your relationships with others. It is important to rid ourselves of the bossy impulse which urges us on to help others cope with their problems in every circumstance. The first thing we have to admit is that we are powerless over other people's lives.'

One point on which some other workers in the field of drug abuse tend to question the Families Anonymous approach is regarding Families Anonymous's apparent approval of the concept known as 'Tough Love'. This involves a last-resort decision to force the addict to leave home unless he is prepared to start treatment. Many consider this too harsh a course for drug-users who are especially vulnerable because of youth, immaturity, poor health or erratic behaviour. By denying the addict food and shelter, parents could be helping to expose him to greater dangers. And this argument applies particularly in the case of young girls.

But there are situations in which you need to get the addict out of the house to save your own sanity and bring him to his senses, parents have admitted. Some of these were Families Anonymous members, others were not.

In one case there was no alternative, a Birmingham mother recalled: 'He was literally impossible – there was no way we could have gone on living in the same house with him as things were. He was mixing heroin and alcohol and slimming pills and anything else he could find, and he was very violent at times. As far as he was concerned no one else had any rights in the family.'

'Usually, you don't get violent behaviour with the younger boy on heroin who doesn't meddle with other drugs,' said a Surrey mother. 'The reason I finally threw my son out was not because his behaviour was threatening in any way, but because he seemed so maddeningly content with things as they were that I couldn't stand it another day. Finally, I allowed him back home although he is still using heroin, but I couldn't bear to see him out on his own during the winter.'

'Tough Love is a very personal matter which each parent must decide for him- or herself,' Sue explained. 'It's a last-ditch measure which wouldn't be suitable in all cases. I had to do it once with my son – it meant refusing money, changing the door locks and so on. It worked because he went straight to a clinic. But it is essential to do it only when the moment seems right.'

In a world where professionals working without adequate back-up support find the treatment of young drug-users such an up-hill struggle, Families Anonymous's reports of the group's many successes might make the task seem relatively easy. Nothing could be further from the truth although finding out about Families Anonymous earlier on in a child's involvement with drugs could be expected to help cut short the long years of misery in a great many cases.

'Before I was helped through FA I was doing all the wrong things. Then I tried a new way and it worked. Today I am well and my daughter is well; and we are both feeling better than we've felt for many years,' said Shelley, recalling the loneliness and unreasoning guilt of earlier years. 'When you have a child using drugs, a lot of people tend to think of it as a moral rather than a health or social problem. So you assume that they think that this has happened because you are a bad parent. It was only through meeting so many parents of addicts who seemed ideal parents in every way that I was finally able to get my own situation into perspective.'

Shelley's daughter was fourteen when she began using drugs. Now she is 22 and has been drug-free for over two years.

'She started sniffing glue and swallowing an assortment of pills, smoking pot, injecting heroin, taking Diconal and other prescribed drugs. By the time she was seventeen she was very "street-wise" in that she knew how to survive around London's illicit drugs culture. She was getting prescriptions for drugs like Diconal from about five doctors in different areas at one time. Then she would take these down to the Dilly [Piccadilly Circus] and trade some of them in for heroin.

'I think the first time that it really hit me was one day when I gave her money to buy some clothes and she came back as high as a kite. Then the nightmare began. Eventually, she became very ill with hepatitis and other complaints. Her weight was down to just over six stone, which was very low for a tall girl. She was literally at death's door, and there didn't seem to be anything I could do to help. By this time she had been arrested on numerous occasions, and nothing seemed to make any difference to her. It was a question of waiting for the next blow to fall, and feeling completely helpless.

'Then I heard of Families Anonymous, and it changed everything. I discovered that even if I couldn't change my daughter's life, I could change my own life. From then on I changed my entire attitude. I told her that she must never again ask me for money to buy drugs. In the beginning I was going out to meetings twice a week, and in the end I was going nearly every day. It was a tremendous shake-up for her to find that attention was being diverted away from her, and that I was no longer prepared to sit and wait at home. Addicts don't like this sort of situation – they get into the habit of being the centre of attention with the activities of the entire family revolving around them.

'Although I was feeling much stronger, her behaviour wasn't improving. Indeed, it got so bad at one stage that living with her became unbearable. A time came when she was arrested after she had stolen what amounted to thousands of pounds from us and we thought that she didn't have long to live. So we told her we would prosecute and let her go to prison. The police held her for two days. Then they let her go and she went out that night and was arrested again. When she came home she said she would go to a clinic, although she had always been unwilling to have treatment before.

'When it came to the point she wasn't willing to go on this occasion either. So I forced her physically into the car, and gave her some methadone which I had managed to get from my own doctor for this purpose. Then I drove for four-and-a-half hours to reach Broadway Lodge in Weston-super-Mare, which is a private residential centre where they use the same twelve-step programme as Families Anonymous and Narcotics Anonymous. She was there for four weeks, and she has never looked back.

'Of course I'm well aware that she need not have gone on the programme, had she not chosen to let me bully her into it. I believe that in her heart she was ready to change her life. And I'm happy that she has come through it all with her personality intact, and still the lovable person she always was when she wasn't using drugs. I've discovered that most addicts have very nice personalities, and are basically intelligent, caring people. Perhaps they are in some way more vulnerable.

'Another thing I've discovered is that parents who are most successful in helping their children through problems of any kind are the ones who mean "no" when they say "no". It is much harder to do this, but it can make all the difference. I wish I'd known about Families Anonymous and its philosophy when my children were younger. I hope many other parents can learn through my experience.'

Meanwhile, as the current increase in drug abuse among young people continues to escalate, more and more parents are being referred to Families Anonymous by doctors, nurses, social workers, voluntary agencies and the police. 'What help can police offer? What do you tell a parent, a wife, a husband, whose world has just fallen apart?' asks a special feature in the Force's own journal, *The Job*.

The answer is to be found in just two words, 'Families Anonymous', says Chief Inspector Dick Stacey. 'We are in the front line. We see more people in this kind of trouble than most. We also seek to be a caring agency – not just a force which deals with crime but with its effects as well. Those effects on the families can be shattering . . . Helping is as much part of our job as detection.'

Yet another striking success story is included in the police report. In this case a middle-aged businessman had discovered eighteen months previously that his designer son was support-ing a £200-a-week heroin habit. And so was the young man's fiancée who shared his flat. Then early one morning the father received a telephone call to say their flat was surrounded by police. This turned out to be an hallucination, but it did result in the young couple splitting up and returning to their respec-tive parents.

Though the story ended happily with the son seeking volun-tary admission to a clinic and eventually returning to work, it was only through joining Families Anonymous that the parents learned how best to offer support without interference, until the young man was ready to be helped.

'I think at the time Families Anonymous probably helped my wife more than it did me,' the father recalled with a flash of humour. 'At least it helped her to stop thinking she was the only Jewish mother in North London whose son was an addict.'

The Families Anonymous programme 'Twelve Steps' fol-lows. Families Anonymous points out that the programme is spiritual, not religious, and that participants are free to use their own private interpretation of the phrase 'a Power greater than ourselves' in all Twelve Steps programmes.

Families Anonymous Twelve Steps
We have found that our success in this programme is deter-mined by how well we accept and apply the following suggested steps:
1. Admitted we were powerless over drugs and other people's lives – that *our* lives had become unmanageable.
2. Came to believe that a Power greater than ourselves could restore us to sanity.
3. Made a decision to turn our will and our lives over to the care of God, *as we understood Him.*

126

4. Made a searching and fearless moral inventory of ourselves.
5. Admitted to God, to ourselves and to another human being the exact nature of our wrongs.
6. Were entirely ready to have God remove all these defects of character.
7. Humbly asked Him to remove our shortcomings.
8. Made a list of all persons we had harmed, and became willing to make amends to them all.
9. Made direct amends to such people whenever possible, except when to do so would injure them or others.
10. Continued to take personal inventory and when we were wrong promptly admitted it.
11. Sought through prayer and meditation to improve our conscious contact with God as we understood Him, praying only for knowledge of His will for us and the power to carry that out.
12. Having had a spiritual awakening as a result of these steps, we tried to carry this message to others and to practise these principles in all our affairs.

OTHER PROFESSIONALS

One of the most disturbing impressions one receives from talking to parents is the idea that the family doctor has no place in this situation.

'Derek wouldn't want it and the doctor wouldn't be interested. Besides, it's something he brought on himself – not an illness that it might seem reasonable to call the doctor out in the middle of the night for,' said one mother, describing one frightening occasion when her son's breathing became difficult during a period of withdrawal.

Derek has since been diagnosed as asthmatic, and he has given up drugs apart from prescribed medicines for his condition. This case underlines the danger of attributing all sorts of physical symptoms to the effects of drug abuse. For those with a light habit it may be relatively easy to go through a withdrawal phase, but, as experts increasingly advise, you have to look at the entire person, including all his strengths and weaknesses.

127

This holistic approach applies to the individual's general health, too.

Parents need to get away from the idea that drug-taking and associated problems are something the youngster 'brought on himself'. If this argument were to be followed to its logical conclusion, then vast sums of public money would not be spent on the prevention and treatment of illnesses associated with smoking and alcoholism, which occur in adult life. By contrast, the teenager caught up in an illicit drug-taking culture bears far less responsibility for his own condition.

Under the National Health Service, everyone is entitled to general medical services through a GP. It is the responsibility of parents to ensure that their offspring are registered with a GP, who is contracted to the Department of Health and Social Security to provide a service for patients on his, or her, list. In ordinary circumstances, parents take responsibility for recognizing the need for a medical opinion when a child appears ill; this responsibility must also apply to any worrying symptom associated with drug abuse.

In the ordinary way you would call the doctor if you noticed that your child's breathing was very rapid, laboured or noisy; if he were retching or vomiting continually; if he were suffering from a combination of diarrhoea and vomiting for several hours (which brings a risk of dehydration); if he seemed unusually drowsy and difficult to rouse; if he were in severe pain or running a high temperature (e.g. of 101°F/38.4°C or over, with chest symptoms or severe pain); if there were some worrying skin sign such as a severe rash or blueness of the face (cyanosis), which might indicate breathing difficulties.

You do not have to think twice about what to do in an acute emergency such as an overdose: call an ambulance or drive to the nearest general hospital. Thankfully, such crises are said to be quite rare with younger drug-users. The more likely situation is one in which an anxious parent feels that a doctor should be called but hesitates. The sensible thing to do is to go ahead and call the doctor if you are really worried. Keep your patient warm, and do not give anything by mouth while you wait if there is vomiting or abdominal pain. And do not feel embarrassed about calling *your* doctor out in the middle of the night when necessary. The chances are that you will receive a visit from a deputizing doctor, for these help to provide the nation with a 24-hour family doctor service.

For the majority of adolescent drug-users (especially those aged sixteen years and under), residential treatment is not thought to be essential, except where there are additional physical or emotional problems calling for special attention. As Dr Judith Morgan points out, the young person's problem and its solution need to be seen in the context of family and home community. And as many observers have said, there is no magical cure which will change the youngster's life for the better overnight. Neither is there one treatment strategy which is better than all the others for everyone.

Perhaps the most important lesson that parents of drug-users can learn is one which all professionals emphasize: you will not get anywhere with treating the youngster until he or she is ready to make a sincere effort to stop using the drug. It goes without saying that you will worry, but try not to worry about this aspect. It is not your fault that your child turned to drugs in the first place when his classmates were involved, too; and it is not your fault if you just cannot make him start a cure.

What you can do, of course, is to encourage your child to make use of any help available locally which will guide him in the direction of greater insight into his own problems. In most areas this can be found through a drugs counselling service, and fortunately these services are increasing. Another way for an adolescent to learn more about himself and his motivation is through group work, which is available through hospital clinics and many voluntary organizations which provide therapy. In this case a group of people sharing the same sort of problem explores its attitudes and feelings with the guidance of a therapist.

In terms of the kind of therapy approach which is likely to be most helpful, the average young drug-user tends to be seen as immature for his age, withdrawn, lacking in self-confidence, having poor self-esteem and little in the way of self-assertiveness. These are the sorts of characteristics which used to be applied to someone described as 'easily led', but when you come to think of it, most people are easily led when they are young and vulnerable and faced with the opportunity to experiment.

For a great many of us, yielding to that challenge meant lighting up a first cigarette and going through years of what seemed at the time a harmless enough addiction. In fact, according to a 1980 report in the *Health Education Journal,* smokers have a lot in common with drug-abusers: 'Research studies have indicated that cigarette-smokers have specific personality characteristics which are significantly different from those of non-smokers. Susceptibility to peer pressure and conformity were highly correlated with the initiation and continuation of cigarette-smoking,' wrote Dr Linda Del Greco of Bridgewater State College, Massachusetts.

More recent research by Professor Denise Candell of Columbia University seems to suggest that for most of us there is a vulnerable stage in the teens, with a cut-off point at 22 years, during which there is enhanced susceptibility to habit-forming substances. According to this study, a person who has not used alcohol, drugs or cigarettes by the age of 22 is unlikely to use them in future. On the other hand, there is evidence that many young heroin-users have also used solvents and other drugs at an earlier stage, as well as alcohol and cigarettes.

But if personality plays some small part in the development of a drug habit, availability is a very potent factor as many observers, including research psychologist Dr Michael Gossop, have stressed. Theories as to whether a particular type of personality or home background is more likely to encourage a tendency to drug-addiction have failed, he claims. He cites the higher-than-average incidence of addicts among doctors and nurses, especially in the United States, as evidence supporting the view that availability is a crucial factor.

While some young addicts come from homes in which family relationships have been disturbed for a long time, many do not. What does seem indisputable is that disturbed family relationships are common in the families of young addicts, which is a very different matter. A truism often heard in a different context is that 'the family with a handicapped person in it is a handicapped family'. If we take the term 'handicapped' to apply broadly, not only to conditions of physical and mental disability but also to problems such as alcoholism and drug abuse, it is not difficult to see how continuously disruptive behaviour on the part of one member could undermine the family's emotional stability. This is very obvious from what the parents who contributed to this book have said.

When it comes to treating the young drug-user, however, the need to work with the family is seen as paramount, whether the habit grew out of difficult personal relationships, a vulnerable personality, availability of the drug or the persuasion of companions – or a combination of all of these. Even where parents manage to remain tolerant, relationships with brothers and sisters may have deteriorated badly due to unacceptable behaviour on the drug-user's part. The task of the counsellor or therapist is to help bring the family together as a unit while working with the young person, usually on an individual basis.

There are many different techniques which have proved successful in helping young people to turn away from drugs and take control of their own lives. Some of these are forms of therapy which have been developed in the United States, where experience with the problem of teenage drug abuse on a large scale dates back much farther than it does in Britain. For instance, a recently published official survey of 27,414 New York children showed that more than 30 per cent of 12- and 13-year-olds admitted having used drugs illicitly. This showed only a small increase over a five-year period, although the types of drugs used had varied considerably. No one knows what percentage of children of a similar age in cities such as London, Liverpool or Glasgow are using drugs either regularly or occasionally, but the figure is thought to be very much lower than that of New York.

One of the techniques widely used in helping young people with a drug problem is assertiveness-training, which is an element in all group therapy, or can be part of a teaching programme. Most of those who benefit from assertiveness-training in the United States, and increasingly in Britain, do not have drug-abuse problems. They are more likely to be shy, lack self-confidence, and feel depressed and ineffectual because they are unable to make their point of view heard. They find that they cannot stand up for their own rights – in personal relationships or in their employment – without showing anger and hostility. So they tend to react passively, allowing themselves to be persuaded against their will, rather than risk an unpleasant confrontation by saying no.

In the treatment of drug abuse, assertiveness-training encourages the withdrawn youngster with low self-esteem to learn to 'speak his mind' confidently as well as to listen to the views of others with a similar problem. Gradually, as he gains self-confidence, he learns that he has a will of his own, that his views are worthy of respect, and that there are choices which he can make – the most important being whether to continue using drugs or to stop and think more positively about his future.

Any therapy programme which boosts morale and helps the youngster gain more insight into his own motivation is bound to be beneficial, even if it does not immediately lead to an end to drug abuse. The consensus among professionals working in this field is that successfully weaning a young person away from drugs – once he has taken the essential first step of deciding that he wants to stop – can be an agonizingly slow process. And it is here that involving the family in the treatment philosophy can be crucial.

THE VOLUNTARY AGENCY: TURNING POINT
Of the many non-statutory organizations providing valuable help for people with drug problems, one of the longest-established is Turning Point. This has operated for over twenty years, and was known originally as the Helping Hand Organization.

Turning Point is an 'umbrella' organization, which currently has responsibility for 21 separate projects and five attached services, which include group homes and flatlets. Of the 21 projects, five are for people at various stages of problem drug-taking. Two are mental health projects, and the rest are for people with alcohol problems. There are two regional offices, in London and Manchester.

The diversity of the programme for drug-users can be gauged from the following list of projects. They include Suffolk House, a 'concept house' opened in 1969 (concept houses are discussed on pages 108 and 109); the Hungerford Drug Project, which

132

was set up in 1970 as a day facility providing easy 'street access' to young people with drug problems. Roma, which was taken over by Turning Point in 1980, is a residential rehabilitation centre for notified drug-users who are receiving a medically prescribed drug, such as methadone. (At present, this is usually given as a 'reduction prescription' to help the person become drug-free gradually.) Birmingham Drugline and Sheffield Drugline offer information and counselling to problem drug-users and their relatives.

Of particular interest because of the new initiatives being launched in 1985 is the Hungerford Drug Project, which is based in Craven Street, near Trafalgar Square, in London. It provides a drop-in information service and also has an appointments system for assessment and referrals. Now, with the help of a grant from the Mental Health Foundation, the Hungerford is appointing a detached youth worker, one of whose jobs will be to go out and make contact with young people with drug problems in the places around London where they are likely to congregate, rather than waiting in the hope that they will eventually find their way to the centre. A fourth full-time social worker is also being appointed.

'The background to this new youth project dates back to 1981,' explained Janis Barrett, regional director for the South of England, 'when people working in the drugs field noticed a sudden increase in the number of young people from working-class areas who were getting into difficulties through smoking heroin. In Islington it was noted that the age of working-class youths using heroin had dropped to thirteen and fourteen years old. Our own figures for 16-25-year-olds showed an increasing number of younger people. We had a 50 per cent increase in the total number of new referrals in 1982 and again in 1983. And in each year approximately half were aged 25 or younger. Yet up to about two years ago, most Hungerford clients were in the 24–30 age-range.'

Hungerford records reflect changes in the pattern of drug use in line with those reported elsewhere in Britain. Its figures for 1984 show that heroin was by far the most frequently used drug among clients in the four weeks before they made contact. In the second quarter of 1984, 48 per cent of clients had used heroin; 15 per cent used other opiates; 11 per cent used stimulants; 14 per cent used sedative/hypnotics; 4 per cent used other drugs; and 8 per cent were drug-free.

'We find that between 60 and 70 per cent of Hungerford clients are now opiate-users; and between 10 and 15 per cent are using tranquillizers (compared with about 40 per cent of those who telephone to Birmingham Drugline, of which a high proportion are women).

'In the past we have found that we do not see most of the younger people until they have a well established pattern of drug-taking, and are beginning to worry about it. At this stage most of them will have had no contact whatever with a helping agency, and some will have only a very superficial understanding of the drugs they have been using. We see this as a potentially dangerous situation, and it is a difficult one to deal with unless you can make contact with people at a much earlier stage than at present. This is where our new project with a detached youth worker should make a big difference.

'One of our aims is to intervene in such a way that we can reduce harm to the young person through disseminating information. Some people may see harm-reduction information as a form of collusion with drug use; but we believe that clients should be given information which they need to prevent damaging side-effects. For example, if they inject – which many still do – they may not realize that it makes a difference if you use clean needles. It's not collusion to try to prevent liver damage or repeated abscesses, which hospital casualty department staff would rather not have to treat anyway.'

The new Hungerford project will have two principal aims, Janis Barrett explained. Firstly, it will provide a direct service for people in the 16–25 age-range, with enough flexibility to help some people younger or older than the stipulated limit. In the main it is anticipated that those being helped will not be long-established drug-users; and that older drug-users with a long-standing problem will be referred to office-based workers at the Hungerford Drug Project, who will be working closely with the detached youth worker.

Another objective will be the gathering of information to enable Turning Point to build up a profile of the overall drug problem involving younger people, so that a clearer picture of the nature of the current need for services will emerge. 'What we discover will have implications for the development of appropriate services. For example, if we find that young drug-users are mainly homeless, then we could be thinking in terms of a residential facility. If we find that most of them have full-time jobs, this would indicate a need for an evening service.

'Under these broad headings, we hope it will be possible to be more innovative in the way we deal with young people who don't have a well-established drug pattern. We hope to be able to demystify the drug problem, at least at this level of use, and that non-specialist agencies can be encouraged to take on young people. What most of these new younger drug-takers are likely to need are good youth services, rather than services for people with drug problems. It is our view that people with drug problems usually experience a range of social problems such as breakdown of relationships, unemployment, homelessness, legal problems, health problems and so on.

'At present there are no residential rehabilitation facilities which cater specifically for the needs of the younger drug-user and people with recently established drug problems. Existing therapeutic communities are geared towards the needs of clients with entrenched problems which may have started in adolescence but have persisted well beyond. While there is no doubt about the value of these programmes in helping some people to stay off drugs, it is widely acknowledged that the therapeutic community model of treatment doesn't suit the needs of all drug-users, particularly younger people and those at an early stage in a career of drug misuse.

'Experience in working with this younger client group suggests that existing rehabilitation facilities are often inappropriate and unappealing to the less established drug-user. Their needs are different in that their decision to seek help is more likely to have been precipitated by a crisis, rather than through disillusionment with their current lifestyle. Consequently, unless their interest can be engaged fairly quickly through more rewarding and fulfilling experiences, drug-taking is likely to retain much of its attraction.'

The new project should also enable Turning Point to

improve on one of the tasks which it carries out already. This is to monitor trends in drug use, and to pass this information on to clients and key agencies. For instance, it may be discovered that the heroin for street distribution is being mixed with some other noxious substance, and it is essential for information about this risk to be made known to everyone involved.

Janis Barrett continued: 'Because our new project will be based entirely in the London area, we are likely to have a much more transient clientele than you would expect to find in a provincial centre. We won't be confining our intervention to the West End only, though you still tend to see a lot more younger users around the Piccadilly area during the summer. While the London drug culture has tended to disperse to areas like Earl's Court and King's Cross, we are not starting out with preconceived ideas about where younger users are to be found. We just don't know at present.'

Another project being set up by Turning Point in 1985 is a much needed drug-free rehabilitation house with accommodation for 30 residents in West Bromwich. It is hoped that this will be funded by a grant from the government's three-year programme to counter the problem of drug-abuse. As there is no other rehabilitation centre in the West Midlands, it is expected that most referrals will come initially from All Saints Hospital, Birmingham. The staff will have the back-up support of a community nurse and a visiting GP, and possibly a medical consultant.

'The project will be structured to provide a framework in which rehabilitation can operate effectively, but there will be nothing as strict as a behaviourist approach with a system of rewards and punishments to encourage co-operation,' Ms Barrett explained. 'What we want to achieve is a rewarding, stimulating and community-orientated environment which goes beyond traditional occupational therapy activities like gardening, to engage the interest of young people who come for help at a time of crisis in their lives. We will therefore place a lot of emphasis on education, training, the development of leisure interests – and we hope to be able to arrange sessional visits by teachers with special skills.

'The content of the programme will emphasize the development of personal resources, through which people can take responsibility for changing their lifestyles once they leave the programme. The centre's activities will also be designed to promote involvement in the community to which people intend to return. These will include counselling, group-work (geared to examining issues such as self-image, gaining confidence, assertiveness, assessing and responding to the needs of others), group living, learning to take responsibility for their own lives.

'The programme will place considerable emphasis on seeking and securing training and employment, including voluntary work. In a climate of high unemployment, developing leisure interests is seen as a very important aspect of the programme. The centre will have workshop facilities where people can learn arts, crafts and so on; and it is envisaged that "activities workers" – backed up by skilled sessional workers – will help provide a wide range of activities, including music, drama, dance, relaxation and sport. An active interest in topical issues will be encouraged through discussion with public representatives and others invited to the centre by the resident group. Greater emphasis will be placed on working with families. A self-help group for parents and relatives of residents will be run in collaboration with Birmingham Drugline.'

Janis Barrett's own practical experience in this field began with a five-year stint in a very different type of residential setting: with another Turning Point project, Roma, which is Britain's only facility to offer residential support to notified drug-users who are receiving a prescription from a GP or drug-treatment centre.

'Reduction prescribing can have a valuable role to play where it is being used to provide a breathing space while people make decisions about their future. I think it is important to stress this aspect – where the aim is to provide an opportunity for people to take the first step in working towards a drug-free lifestyle. I am also in favour of giving people who have failed in this regime the opportunity to try again. I don't doubt that for some people a maintenance prescription may work, but in my personal experience of working with people receiving prescriptions I have seen little evidence to support this. I believe that for many it creates a climate of pessimism in which they cease to believe that they can change their lifestyle.

'What made helping drug-takers such a difficult management problem some years ago was the fact that many people were using barbiturates. These figure less and less in the problems we see nowadays, although we come across a sudden increase from time to time. The public never became really concerned about barbiturates – perhaps because these were drugs which doctors prescribed – and yet they were far more dangerous than heroin. People reach crisis-point much more rapidly with barbiturates. And once they have an established dependency, it is dangerous for them to stop without medical supervision, because withdrawal can result in severe epilepsy-type fits. It is much easier to overdose with barbiturates too. A substantial number of our clients died through barbiturate overdose when these were readily available and widely used, although most of them had been using drugs for an average of ten years at the time. Since then very few Roma residents have died as a result of overdose.'

Today, Roma is a much more dynamic centre, offering a structured programme of counselling and group work through which residents acquire skills and gather information which will broaden their range of choices and help them to make decisions about their future lives.

People coming to Roma are usually homeless, unemployed, isolated and in poor health. It has been shown that the average length of time using drugs among Roma clients is about fifteen years, which is considerably higher than anywhere else. Progress tends to be slow, because entry to Roma usually marks the beginning of a long process towards rehabilitation.

'The work of a centre like Roma involves a long-term commitment. One rarely witnesses "success" as the term is usually understood. In this context, success is also difficult to define and even more difficult to measure. A socially accepted goal both for the drug-taker and the public at large may be the attainment of a job and a home. But in reality, such arrangements are likely to break down without friendships and relationships. The point is that a wide range of practical and emotional problems have to be tackled, and people have to learn new strategies for coping with these problems. If I were to think in terms of progress in a particular case, I might be talking about someone who has been having treatment for about five years, and whose treatment is still continuing.'

Speaking at the annual conference of the Mental Health Foundation in November 1984, Janis Barrett had some harsh criticisms to make against irresponsible media coverage of the current heroin problem. She did acknowledge, however, that something positive had been achieved through this publicity – the awakening of public conscience. And another bonus was the growing public understanding of what it meant to have a drug problem: 'People are becoming increasingly aware that people with drug problems just might turn out to be people like us . . . our relatives . . . our friends.'

But as she points out, increased public concern has not been paralleled by a marked improvement in services for people with drug problems. Indeed, the critical shortage of suitable facilities was highlighted in Turning Point's 1983–4 report, which described the unsuccessful efforts of one Hungerford client and its staff to arrange for professional counselling. The prospect of a three-month wait became too much in the end, and the client began using drugs again. Happily, there are many other stories which end on a more optimistic note.

6 The police and the drugs problem

Permission was given by the Metropolitan Police Authority at New Scotland Yard for interviews with police officers working in a South London District Drugs Unit. Owing to the need for confidentiality, neither their names nor their precise area of work can be identified. Readers are reminded that members of the public can telephone the police with confidential information on their 24-hour Anonymous Drugs Line: 01–230 2121.

A Detective Sergeant with the District Drugs Unit
'This unit was set up in June 1984 as a purpose-built unit, with staff who already had an interest in the problem of drug abuse in the local area. We have a total of eleven officers, including three sergeants, two women police constables and six male police constables. We could employ at least forty people full-time in this area alone to cope with all the work that needs to be done. At the same time, it needs to be said that there is very much more police activity in this area now than there was nine months ago.

'Our brief is to aim at catching the suppliers of drugs – especially heroin – at street level. Of the 250 arrests we have made so far, 90 per cent were for heroin offences. We receive information from many different sources, including the new Anonymous Drugs Line. Obviously, we have to be very careful about cross-checking anonymous information. Sometimes we get parents ringing up to tell us about their own children being involved with drugs. [In such cases] we find that family support groups can be very helpful. On other occasions a neighbour may call to say that someone down the road seems to have more money to spend than can be accounted for, and that he might be selling drugs.

140

'I carry around in my head the addresses of about a dozen street dealers, and other officers will be able to come up with at least twenty names of people we know are involved. We will know quite a lot about them, but they won't know us by sight. We don't take anyone to court until we have a strong case, and this means that we have a high conviction rate. In terms of sentencing we are getting very good support from the courts. The minimum for street-level dealers is three years, and the maximum is six years.

'Because our energies are directed towards dealers rather than users, we haven't come in contact with many young people in serious trouble through drugs. Of the 250 people we arrested since we began work in the unit, only four were juveniles. We get a great many calls from parents for help, however, and when I'm talking about their children I may well be thinking in terms of people in their twenties.

'For instance, I know of one young man who is a 28-year-old heroin-user, and his parents have placed him under house arrest. While his father is at work during the day, he stays indoors with his mother. He came very close to going to prison at one stage. Now he is prepared to accept close parental supervision.

'Naturally, we take a personal interest in many of the people we meet. We are always encouraged when young people seem to be beating the habit. There are three cases which come to mind of young people who left London to give up heroin and settle back in their own communities. And when they seemed to have succeeded, they returned to London and each of them in turn went straight back on to heroin again.

'One of the saddest cases I know involves a 24-year-old woman who has been on drugs since she was fourteen and on heroin for the past four or five years. After a period of smoking heroin she went on to injecting, and on one occasion she was sold a supply of heroin mixed with yeast. As a result of this she is now blind in one eye, and the sight in her other eye is also affected; she is also partially paralysed on one side of her body.

'At any given time we are likely to be taking an interest in the welfare of a number of patients in certain teaching hospitals. A recent tragedy involved a Nigerian lady in her thirties who

141

arrived unexpectedly to stay with friends on the day she entered the United Kingdom. When they came home from work they found her in a coma and had her admitted to hospital, where her blood was found to have a very high concentration of morphine. Since heroin is converted to morphine in the body, this indicated a massive overdose of heroin.

'The explanation was that she had been smuggling heroin into the country in her digestive tract. Instead of being packed in the contraceptive sheaths most smugglers use for this purpose, the heroin she had swallowed was wrapped in non-waterproof material. Consequently, when her digestive secretions or fluid she drank soaked through the wrapping, the drug was absorbed into her bloodstream.

This lady survived for six days after her collapse. We recovered 25 folds of heroin from her body, which contained heroin worth about £12,000 on the basis of the current street price of £80 a gram. Incidentally, the world record for heroin carried this way stands at 300 "lumps". Why do people take such risks? It is very tempting when people are offered a substantial amount of money to smuggle something. What they don't realize is how dangerous it is to swallow powerful narcotics, even if they seem to be well wrapped.

'About 80 per cent of the heroin coming into the country now originates in Pakistan. This is the brown "diamorphine base" powder, which we've been getting for only about four or five years. This is usually smoked, and cannot be injected unless it is dissolved in a particular medium. Earlier, when most of the heroin reaching us was coming from Thailand, it was in the form of white "diamorphine hydrochloride" powder, which was injectable but couldn't be smoked. In this way, sources of supply determine the pattern of drug use at a given time.

'Sometimes it is possible to lose sight of the fact that other drugs given as substitutes for heroin can also be dangerous both to users and, if left accessible, to children. A case in point is methadone – a synthetic opiate often prescribed to wean people off heroin. This is as addictive as heroin, and withdrawal from it is more severe. Most authorities say that you can withdraw physically from heroin in between one and two weeks, but with methadone withdrawal can take up to three months. Some

142

doctors now say that if reduction-prescribing is necessary, then it is safer to use heroin. Obviously, this is a controversial argument, as an increasing number of doctors are opposed to the use of drugs in treatment.

'Recently, for the first time, we heard that the price of heroin had gone up to £100 a gram (from £80). It is too soon yet to say if this marks the beginning of a pattern reflecting a scarcity of the drug, perhaps associated with increasing police activity in this area. Different patterns tend to emerge in various parts of the country, depending on supply and demand. In the King's Cross area of London, for instance, there is a big trade involving dealers from Ireland, who buy heroin at £80 a gram and re-sell it at street level in Dublin for about £300 a gram. Even at that price, Dublin has a very serious heroin problem.'

A District Inspector in charge of a District Drugs Unit
'There are no reliable police statistics on drugs so far. Drugs do not feature as a problem in criminal statistics until the police become active and make arrests. An area where there is a lot of police activity will appear to have a greater drugs problem than another where there is less activity. This means that you can easily get a biased view of what is happening in a specific area.

'The Metropolitan Police Commissioner's initiatives for 1985 are against racial attacks and drugs, so this means that much more priority is being given to the fight against drug abuse.

'The position in South London at present is rather like that of a man crossing a river: he knows it is deep, but he doesn't know how deep it is. We have a great deal of work to do and we have a lot more information than we can cope with – if we had three times our present number of staff we wouldn't have enough. Another problem is the increase in crime associated with finding money to support a habit with an average cost of £250–£350 a week.

'Our efforts are directed towards street dealers, not towards users. But sometimes a distraught father or mother will ask us to pick up a user, and we may do this. However, we take the view generally that to arrest a user in possession of a small amount of heroin is not going to be helpful. Even if we take him before the courts, the resources are not available to the courts to ensure that he can go somewhere where he can be weaned off drugs.

'On the other hand, there are times when we have to arrest users in order to get evidence against pushers. We find that a very high percentage of dealers are unemployed and drawing unemployment benefit. Most appear not to have anything much in terms of wealth. In fact, the majority only subsist themselves by dealing in drugs, or by resorting to prostitution or other crimes. The typical pusher tends to live in squalid conditions because of his lifestyle, but as far as external appearances are concerned, he is just an ordinary bloke who might be living anywhere – perhaps next-door. One dealer was living at home with his parents, who just thought he was very popular because he seemed to have so many friends calling!

'In our unit we have to limit our enquiries to street dealers. The work of all the different metropolitan units is co-ordinated through the Central Drugs Squad, which has a staff of 30–40 officers attached to Scotland Yard. Street dealers tend to have many contacts and to trade between themselves. There are likely to be several middle-men between the pusher and the importer, for whom drug-trafficking is a very lucrative low-risk, high-return enterprise.

'One of the problems which the police encounter in the ordinary way is that people tend to see them as authoritarian. Yet there was a time when they had a recognized role rather like that of a community worker. One of the more positive spin-offs associated with the current drug problem is that a closer relationship is developing and we are getting full support from everyone. Perhaps this is because we are one of the few agencies which can be seen to be going something about it.

'The situation at the moment is that if we were to arrest all the drug-users we found and refer them to the few services which are available, we would swamp them immediately. When we do arrest them, and they are willing to go for treatment in the hope of getting the charge mitigated, the only realistic advice we can give them is that they should try for treatment at a private clinic. We find that voluntary groups also play a very valuable part – although they don't have enough resources – because they have street-credibility as far as the users are concerned.

'It is sad that the National Health Service seems to have so little to offer at this level. But I know that if I say to someone, "You go and see your GP," the best he can hope for is to get on a waiting-list; it could take at least three months before he gets an appointment to see someone.' In such circumstances, breaking the habit becomes less likely.

'Yet if we could refer people straight away, there would be a good chance that something could be done. There are a few social workers who take a special interest in people with drug problems, but they don't appear to have the resources to offer much help.

'One of the most hopeful developments is that several areas, including our area, have begun discussions to see how we can establish the Multi-Agency Approach to the drug problem, which the DHSS urged in a circular sent out to statutory authorities in June 1984. In this area it has been agreed that we would get together under the auspices of the local health authority. So we have set up a joint committee with representatives from the police, and health, education, social services and housing departments of the local authority.

'So far, an approach on three levels has been agreed. We need an education and prevention programme. We need a drop-in street agency. We need a drug dependency unit with day or residential facilities. The problem when it comes to putting these proposals into practice is money, of course. To set up a street agency capable of dealing with the problem in our area would cost an estimated £2 million for housing, staff and running expenses.

'Meanwhile, we can as yet only guess about the size of the problem out there, waiting for something to be done. We have the impression so far that reports about younger and younger children being involved in heroin abuse have tended to be exaggerated. On the other hand, we see little reason for optimism in the current switch from injecting to smoking heroin. What seems to be happening is that youngsters who would normally be frightened of the needle are more easily persuaded to smoke the drug, especially if it seems the fashionable thing to do.

'If a parent were to ask me, "What is the best way to help

145

protect my child against the risk of involvement in drug abuse?" I would say, "Try to have as close and loving a relationship as possible with your child." The Recorder of London has said that social enquiry reports in respect of people he tried on drugs charges showed that they seemed to have two factors in common: lack of parental love and lack of parental discipline. No doubt there are other factors at work too, including availability of the drug, but this is a thought well worth bearing in mind.'

Help and information services

The addresses of services and sources of information and help listed below are based mainly on information provided by the Standing Conference on Drug Abuse (SCODA).

National organizations
SCODA (Standing Conference on Drug Abuse), 1/4 Hatton Place, Hatton Garden, London EC1N 8ND; tel. 01–430 2341/2. Information about services in all areas.
ISDD (Institute for the Study of Drug Dependence), 1/4 Hatton Place, Hatton Garden, London EC1N 8ND; tel. 01–430 2341/2. Library, information service, teaching materials, literature.
HEALTH EDUCATION COUNCIL, 78 New Oxford Street, London WC1A 1AH; tel. 01–637 1881. Information on local health education services and health campaigns.
MIND (National Association for Mental Health), 22 Harley Street, London W1; tel 01–637 0741. Information and support provided through local associations on matters relating to mental health.
RELEASE, 1 Elgin Avenue, London W9 3PR; tel. 01–289 1123. Advice and referral services, with special emphasis on legal aspects of drug use; 24-hour emergency telephone service on 01–603 8654.
SCOTTISH HEALTH EDUCATION GROUP, Woodburn House, Canaan Lane, Edinburgh EH10 4SG; tel 031 447 8044. Information on local health education services and health-promotion campaigns.

Day projects, information and advisory services
BLENHEIM PROJECT, 7 Thorpe Close, London W10

5XL; tel. 01–960 5599. Advice, information, counselling and support for drug-users, their families and friends.
Appointment necessary. Hours: weekdays, except Wednesday mornings, 10 am–1 pm and 2 pm–5 pm. Tuesday afternoons: women only.
COMMUNITY DRUG PROJECT, 30 Manor Place, London SE17 3BB; tel. 01–703 0559. Social work support, counselling, practical help, referral to other services, home and prison visits for those with drug and drug-related problems in South London. Appointment preferred. Hours: weekdays, except Wednesday afternoons, 10 am–5.30 pm.
HUNGERFORD DRUG PROJECT, First floor, 26 Craven Street, London WC2; tel. 01–930 4688. Advice, support, counselling and referral for those with drug and drug-related problems. Drop-in or appointment service. Hours: weekdays, 2 pm–5 pm, Tuesday, Thursday and Friday, 10 am–1 pm.
LIFELINE PROJECT DAY CENTRE, Joddrell Street, Manchester M3 3HE; tel. 061 832 6353. Support and practical help to drug-users, their families and friends. Assistance with legal problems; assessment and referral for rehabilitation. Advice, information, training and educational facilities for professionals and organizations. Hours: weekdays, 9.30 am– 6 pm.

Specialist advice and information services
ALCOHOL AND DRUGS ADVICE CENTRE, 6 Stanhope Road, South Shields, South Tyneside, Tyne & Wear; tel. South Shields 0632 569 999. Individual counselling and advice on drug and solvent problems. Initial assistance for new self-help groups. Lectures for professionals.
ASHTEAD AND LEATHERHEAD APA, 24 Oakfield Road, Ashtead, Surrey KT22 2RE, tel. 27 73979. Help and support for drug-users, their families and friends. Individual counselling and regular group meetings; 24-hour telephone answering service.
THE BRIDGE PROJECT, Equity Chambers, 40 Piccadilly, Bradford BD1 3NN; tel. 0274 723 863. Advice and counselling.

CADETT, 22 Lansdown Road, London W11; tel. 01–727 9447. Advice, counselling and referral services.

DRUGLINE, Dale House, New Meeting Street, Birmingham 4; tel. 021 632 6363. Telephone counselling and advice for drug-users, their families and friends. Interviews by appointment. Hours: weekdays, 10 am–4 pm. Tuesday, Wednesday, Thursday, 7.30 pm–9.30 pm. Drugline also operates a Family Support Group for parents of solvent-users and a support group for tranquillizer-users.

DRUGSLINE, Room 8, Family Centre, 13 Town Square, Stevenage SG1 1BP; tel. 0438 64067. Advice, information and support.

HERTS AND BEDS STANDING CONFERENCE ON DRUGS MISUSE, Room 8, Family Centre, 13 Town Square, Stevenage SG1 1BP; tel. 0438 315 900. Advice, support and information for drug-users, their families and friends.

MERSEYSIDE DRUGS COUNCIL, 25 Hope Street, Liverpool L1 9BQ; tel. 051 708 0074. Information, advice, counselling and educational programme. Also in Birkenhead.

PAROLE RELEASE SCHEME, 30 Sisters Avenue, London SW11 5SQ; tel. 01–223 2494. Interview and assessment service for drug-dependent prisoners who are eligible for parole; link-up with suitable agencies prior to release. The Scheme also operates a 12-bed minimum support hostel for parolees.

SADD (Solvent Abuse and Drug Dependency), 35–37 Friar Lane, Leicester; tel. 0533 538 926. Advice, counselling and referrals to other services.

SOUTH WALES APA, 111 Cowbridge Road East, Cardiff CF1 9AC; tel. 0222 26113. Nationwide 24-hour counselling service; local education and talks. For details of publications send foolscap-size s.a.e.

DRUG CONCERN (Barnet), 1 Friern Park, North Finchley, London N12; tel. 01–445 5539. Advice and information for drug-users, their families and friends.

SURREY DRUGS RESOURCE SCHEME, 83 East Street, Epsom, Surrey KT17 1DN; tel. 78 29425. Advice, education and training service to professional and voluntary workers in the county. Also runs Surrey Drugline.

149

SURREY DRUGLINE; tel. 78 29266. Telephone advice and information service.
SUBSTANCE ABUSE UNIT, Crossways, Whitehall Road, Uxbridge, Middx; tel. 0895 57285. Information about drugs and solvent abuse.
SOLVENT ABUSE HELPLINE, tel. 01–698 4415. Information and counselling.
NATIONAL CAMPAIGN AGAINST SOLVENT ABUSE; tel. 01–640 2946 or 01–672 1585. Information and counselling through fifteen groups, plus talks to groups.
TRANX (Tranquillizer Recovery and New Existence), 17 Peel Road, Wealdstone, Middlesex HA3 7QX; tel. 01–427 2065. Self-help groups and nationwide contacts.

Non-specialist day projects
BRIDGES, 9a–9b St Albans Road East, Hatfield, Herts; tel. 30 66834. Advisory and counselling service for young people. Day centre with workshop and craft facilities. Can provide emergency accommodation. Hours: Monday, Thursday, Friday, 1.30 pm–7 pm. 24-hour telephone answering service.
KALEIDOSCOPE YOUTH AND COMMUNITY PROJECT, 40–46 Cromwell Road, Kingston-on-Thames, Surrey; tel. 01–549 2681/7488. Community-based project providing advice and recreational facilities for young people. Medical surgery on Friday 10 pm–6 am. The centre includes a hostel with places for 21 young people (aged 16–22) for up to 12 months' rehabilitation. Telephone for information.
NEW HORIZON YOUTH CENTRE, 1 Macklin Street, London WC2; tel. 01–242 0010/2238. Day centre for homeless young people aged 16–25. Advice, counselling and referral services, and assistance with medical, legal and accommodation difficulties. Workshop facilities. Hours: Monday, Tuesday, Wednesday, Friday, 9.30 am–5 pm; Thursday, 9.30 am–1 pm; Sunday afternoons to 5 pm, November–March only.
OPEN DOOR (Hornsey Young People's Consultation Service), 12 Middle Lane, London N8 8PL; tel. 01–384 5947/ 6235. Information, advice, individual counselling and group psychotherapy services for young people aged 13–25. Hours:

Monday to Thursday, 9 am–10 pm; Friday, 9 am–1 pm.
SOHO PROJECT, 142 Charing Cross Road, London WC2;
tel. 01–836 8121. Youth work project offering counselling and
advice to homeless young people in the West End of London.
Hours: Monday-Friday, 10 am–1 pm.
THE UPSTAIRS PROJECT, 182 Hammersmith Road,
London W6; tel. 01–741 3335. Advice, counselling and
activities provided for young people aged 16–25. Hours: drop-
in Monday and Wednesday, 2 pm–6 pm, and Friday, 2 pm–5
pm. Other times by appointment.

Non-specialist information and advisory services
BASEMENT PROJECT, 229 Earls Court Road, London
SW5; tel. 01–373 2335. Advice, information and counselling
for people under 25 years in the Earl's Court area. Hours:
Monday, Thursday, Friday, 10 am–4 pm; Tuesday, 1.30 pm–
4 pm; Wednesday, 2 pm–5 pm.
NUMBER 5 (Young People's Counselling, Advice and
Information Centre), 2–4 Sackville Street, Reading, Berks
RG1 1NT; tel. 0734 585 858. Drug referral point for Reading
Area Health Authority. Provides support and referral to
rehabilitation. No specific age limit. Hours: weekdays 9 am–
10 pm; 24-hour telephone service.
NUCLEUS, 298 Old Brompton Road, London SW5; tel.
01–373 4005.
PICCADILLY ADVICE CENTRE, The Kiosk, Subway 4,
Piccadilly Circus Underground Station, London W1; tel. 01–
930 0066/0140 or 930 0274; and The Office, 9 Archer Street,
London W1; tel. 01–434 3773/3647. Advice and information
on the wide range of problems which may face young people
new to London. Hours: Monday-Thursday, 10 am–9 pm;
Friday-Sunday, 1 pm– 9 pm.
PORTOBELLO PROJECT, 49–51 Porchester Road, London
W2; tel. 01–221 4413/4425. Information and advice for local
young people aged 14–21 on accommodation, drugs,
education, employment, family relationships and medical
problems. Hours: Monday-Friday, 10 am–6 pm.
RELEASE, 1 Elgin Avenue, London W9 3PR; tel. 01–289
1123. National service which provides advice and information

151

on the legal implications of drug use and other problems.
Hours: Monday, Tuesday, Thursday, Friday, 10 am–6 pm.
Provides 24-hour emergency telephone service on 01–603
8654.

Other help services
FESTIVAL WELFARE SERVICES, 347a Upper Street,
London N1 OPD; tel. 01–226 2759. Co-ordinates services of
welfare organizations providing voluntary support for open-air
music festivals throughout Britain; helps with drug problems
and crises; advises on welfare aspects of festival organization.
GREAT CHAPEL STREET MEDICAL CENTRE, 13 Great
Chapel Street, London W1V 7AL; tel. 01–437 9360. Walk-in
medical centre for homeless people of all ages who are not
registered with a family doctor in London. Expert treatment
of drug and alcohol problems. Hours: Monday–Friday, 12
pm–4 pm.
NATIONAL COUNCIL FOR THE WELFARE OF
PRISONERS ABROAD (NCWPA), 347a Upper Street,
London N1 OPD; tel. 01–226 1668. Welfare and information
service for British subjects detained overseas on drug-related
and other criminal charges.

Volunteer support groups and services
BOURNEMOUTH DRUGS ADVISORY SERVICE, 38
Parkstone Road, Poole, Dorset.
CRAWLEY APA, 30 Punchcopse Road, Three Bridges,
Crawley, West Sussex; tel. 0293 22407.
DRUGLINE, 28 Ballina Street, Forest Hill, London SE23
1DR; tel. 01–291 2341. Support and advice for parents of
drug-users.
ELEVENTH HOUR, Gregson Community Centre, Moor
Lane, Lancaster. Meetings: Tuesdays, 7.30 pm–9.30 pm,
support group for users and ex-users; Mondays, 7.30 pm–
9.30 pm, support group for relatives and close friends of
drug-users.
FAMILIES ANONYMOUS, 88 Caledonian Road, London
N1; tel. 01–278 8805. 24-hour telephone answering service.
Personal reply 2 pm–4 pm, Monday-Friday. Advice and

support groups for families and friends of drug-users.
Meetings and contacts in London, Liverpool, Bristol,
Birkenhead, Glasgow, Dublin, Portsmouth, Essex, Bury St
Edmunds. Formation of new groups encouraged.
THE FULHAM CONNECTION, Bishop Creighton House,
378 Lillie Road, London SW6; tel. 01–381 4446. Parents'
meetings on first and third Thursday of month, 7.30 pm.
GODSTONE AND DISTRICT APA, Stoneways, 1 High
Street, Godstone, Surrey; tel. 088 384 842352.
MEDWAY TOWNS DRUG ADVICE SERVICE; tel. 0634
408 755. Mondays, 7.30 pm–9.30 pm.
NARCOTICS ANONYMOUS, PO Box 246, London SW10;
tel. 01–351 6794. Self-help group for drug-users of all ages.
Office usually staffed 2.30 pm–8 pm daily. Meetings and
contacts in London, Liverpool, Bristol, Birkenhead, Dublin
and many other areas. Formation of new groups encouraged.
NORTH WALES ASSOCIATION FOR PREVENTION
OF ADDICTION, 19 Lombard Street, Portmadoc LL49
9AP. Information, advice and support for local drug-users.
PADA (Parents Against Drug Abuse in the Wirral), 142
Home Farm Road, Woodchurch, Birkenhead. Information
centre for parents and relatives of drug-users. Telephone
contact: 051 677 3849.
PARENTS ANONYMOUS, c/o 7 Park Grove, off Broadway,
Worseley, Walkden, Manchester; tel. 061 790 6544. Support
group for families of drug-users.
SAND; tel. (Swansea) 0792 472 002. Telephone service for
drug-users, their families and friends. Hours: Mondays and
Thursdays, 6 pm–10 pm. Also operates self-help group for
people with tranquillizer problems.
SOUTH WALES APA, 111 Cowbridge Road East, Cardiff
CF1 9AG; tel. 0222 26113 24-hour counselling service; wide
network of voluntary helpers.
WEST GLAMORGAN ADVISORY COUNCIL, 36 Orchard
Street, Swansea.

RESIDENTIAL REHABILITATION SERVICES (NON-STATUTORY)
The following categories are included: general houses; concept
houses (work through therapeutic programme); Christian

philosophy (emphasis in varying degrees on acceptance of Christian belief); houses with Christian staff; accommodation for drug-users; crisis centre for multiple-drug-users; non-specialist accommodation; emergency accommodation.

General houses
ALWIN HOUSE, 40 Colville Terrace, London W11; tel. 01–229 0311. For men and women aged 18–24. Voluntary referrals only. Drug-free from day of entry. Long-term accommodation with resident support group and full-time staff.
BRIDGE, Equity Chambers, 40 Piccadilly, Bradford 1; tel. 0274 723 863. For men and women aged 16 and over. 'A relatively unstructured project for chaotic drug-users who want to explore the possibilities facing them.' Accepts residents on bail and conditions of bail. Drug-free on admission.
CRANSTOUN PROJECT, 5 Ember Lane, Esher, Surrey; tel. 01–398 6956. For men aged 20–32. Self-catering democratic community; sheltered workshop; group therapy and individual counselling. Accepts residents on direction of residence orders, not conditions of residence. Drug-free on admission.
CRANSTOUN II, 85 Trinity Road, London SW17; tel. 01–767 7687. For men and women; no age limit. Semi-supportive, relatively unstructured project for residents who have already spent some time in residential rehabilitation, or who have had some form of therapy after withdrawal from drugs. Drug-free on admission.
CRESCENT HOUSE, 10 St Stephen's Crescent, London W2; tel. 01–229 3710. For men and women aged 17 and over. A Richmond Fellowship House providing group therapy and individual counselling. Accepts residents on direction of residence orders, not conditions of residence. Drug-free before admission.
ELIZABETH HOUSE, 94 Redcliffe Gardens, London SW10; tel. 01–370 1279. For men and women aged 24–34. Voluntary referrals only. Drug-free from day of entry. Long-

term accommodation with resident support group. Three full-time staff.
PAROLE RELEASE SCHEME, 30 Sisters Avenue, London
SW11 5SQ; tel. 01–223 2494. For men and women aged 21
and over. A 12-bed minimum-support hostel for drug-
dependent people on parole. Referrals through above address.
235 PROJECT, 235 Balham High Road, London SW17; tel.
01–672 9464. For men and women aged 17 and over. Hostel
for ex-offenders and ex-addicts (drugs/alcohol). This is a
minimum-support unit for use as a stepping-stone to
independent living. Referrals should be drug-free.

Concept houses
ALPHA HOUSE, Wickham Road, Droxford, Southampton
SO3 1PD; tel. 0489 877 210. For men and women aged 16–42.
Drug-free for 24 hours before admission.
INWARD HOUSE, 89 King Street, Lancaster LA1 1RM;
tel. 0524 69599. Men and women aged 16 and over. Drug-free
on admission.
LEY COMMUNITY, Sandy Croft, Sandy Lane, Yarnton,
Oxford; tel. 08675 71777. For men and women. Drug-free for
24 hours before admission.
PHOENIX HOUSE, 1 Eliot Bank, Forest Hill, London
SE23; tel. 01–699 5748/1515. For men and women. Drug-free
for 24 hours before admission.
PHOENIX SHEFFIELD, 229 Graham Road, Ranmoor,
Sheffield S10 3GS; tel. 0742 308 230/391. For men and women
aged 16 and over. Drug-free for 24 hours before admission.
SUFFOLK HOUSE, Long Bridge, Slough Road, Iver Heath,
Bucks; tel. 89 56449. For men and women aged 17 and over.
Drug-free for 48 hours before admission.

Christian philosophy
CHATTERTON HEY, Edenfield, nr. Bury, Lancs; tel. 070
682 3698. For men aged 21–40. Drug-free on admission.
Referrals through Keith Best, Langley House Trust, 26
Heaton Grove, Bradford BD9 4DY; tel. 0274 496 838.
DELIVERANCE INTERNATIONAL, 83 Aldersbrook

Road, London E12; tel. 01–989 4610. For men, preferably under 40. Not required to be drug-free on admission, but must desire to stop using drugs.

META HOUSE (The Bournemouth Project), 133 Princess Road, Westbourne, Bournemouth, Dorset BH4 9HG; tel. 0202 764 581. For women aged 15–35. Drug-free for two weeks before admission. Holding house for up to three months. Residents accepted on conditions of residence.

LIFE FOR THE WORLD TRUST, Oldbury House, Oldbury Court Road, Fishponds, Bristol BS16 2JH; tel. 0272 655 582. For men aged 18–30. Drug-free on admission.

PYE BARN TRUST, 16 The Chase, London SW4; tel. 01–622 4870. For men aged 18–30. Drug-free on admission.

TEEN CHALLENGE, Bryn Road, Penygroes, Llanelli, Dyfed SA14 7PP; tel. (0269) 842 718. For men aged 18 and over. Drug-free on admission; 12-bed hostel based on bible study.

YELDALL MANOR, Hare Hatch, nr. Twyford, Reading, Berks; tel. 073 522 2287. For men aged 18–31. Drug-free on admission; or non-medical withdrawal immediately on admission.

Houses with Christian staff
COKE HOLE TRUST, 70 Junction Road, Andover, Hants; tel. 0264 61045. For men and women aged 16–30. Drug-free on admission. Referrals accepted on conditions of residence from courts.

IDEN MANOR, Staplehurst, Kent; tel. 0580 891 261. For women aged 25–60. Treatment and care for those with problems of *non-opiate* dependency.

STILL WATERS, Nevendon Road, Nevendon, Basildon, Essex SS13 1BY; tel. 0268 726 357. For men and women aged 17–35. 'Extended family home' mainly for young offenders, with priority given to those with addiction problems. Can take a *married* couple with maximum of two children. Will detoxify new admissions.

Accommodation for drug-users
ROMA HOUSE (Turning Point Project), 65–67 Talgarth

Road, London W14; tel. 01–603 8383. For men and women aged 18 and over. Accommodation and care for notified addicts or those in the process of notification. Will consider couples without children. No restriction on referrals.

Crisis centre for multiple drug-users
CITY ROADS (CRISIS INTERVENTION) LTD, 356–358 City Road, London EC1; tel. 01–278 8671. For men and women aged 16–35. Short-stay detoxification for multiple drug-users in crisis. Medical and social work support.

Non-specialist accommodation
INFO, 1 Elmfield Avenue, Stoneygate, Leicester; tel. 0533 709 843. For men and women aged 16–26. People with drug problems considered for admission to this 21-bed hostel for single homeless. Short- or long-term accommodation.
KALEIDOSCOPE, 40–46 Cromwell Road, Kingston-on-Thames, Surrey; tel. 01–549 2681/7488. For men and women aged 16–22. Accommodation for 21 people in cluster flats. Supportive environment offering rehabilitation for people with a variety of problems, including drug misuse.

Emergency accommodation
CENTREPOINT, 57 Dean Street, London W1; tel. 01–734 1075. For men and women aged up to 25, including families. Emergency overnight accommodation. Advice/referral service for homeless people.
HOUSING ADVICE SWITCHBOARD, 47 Charing Cross Road, London WC2H OAN; tel. 01–434 2522/1227. Telephone information service on housing and services for homeless single people and childless couples aged 17–60. Hours: Monday-Friday, 10 am–9 pm; Saturday, 10 am–5 pm.
RIVERPOINT, 229 King Street, London W6; tel. 01–741 2888. Emergency accommodation for men, women and childless couples. Maximum stay 7 nights.

NATIONAL HEALTH SERVICE HOSPITALS PROVIDING SERVICES FOR DRUG-USERS
This list includes clinics which have confirmed to SCODA

157

that they offer some treatment. Some offer only out-patient treatment; some offer only in-patient detoxification; many do not prescribe any drugs. Most hospitals have waiting lists, and operate on a strict catchment-area basis. Many hospitals require new patients to have a referral letter from their own GP. In most cases, services are offered only during certain hours, on an appointment basis.

England

Bedfordshire: Luton & Dunstable Hospital, Dunstable Road, Luton; tel. 0582 53211.

Birkenhead: Arrowe Park Hospital, Upton, Birkenhead; tel. 051 678 5111.

Birmingham: All Saints' Hospital, Lodge Road, Birmingham; tel. 021 523 5151.

Bradford: Waddiloves Hospital, 44 Queen's Road, Bradford; tel. 0274 497121.

Brighton: Drug Dependency Service, 11 Buckingham Road, Brighton; tel. 0273 23395/29604.

Bristol: Glenside Hospital, 20A Blackberry Hill, Stapleton, Bristol; tel. 0272 653285.

Buckinghamshire: St John's Hospital, Stone, Aylesbury; tel. 0296 748 383.

Cambridge: Addenbrookes Hospital, 2 Benett Place, Lensfield Road, Cambridge; tel. 0223 355671 ext. 415.

Cheltenham: Cheltenham General Hospital, Sandford Road, Cheltenham, Gloucester; tel. 0242 580 344.

Chester: (1) Moston Hospital, Upton by Chester; tel. 0244 25202. (2) West Cheshire Hospital, Liverpool Road, Chester; tel. 0244 379333 ext. 314 & 315500 ext. 402.

Devon (South): Moorhaven Hospital, Bittaford, Ivybridge; tel. 07554 2411.

Dorset: St Anne's Hospital, Haven Road, Canford Cliffs, Poole; tel. (0202)708881.

Essex: Runwell Hospital, Wickford, Essex; tel. 03744 5555 ext. 271.

Herts: (1) Hill End Hospital, Hill End Lane, St Albans; tel. 0727 55555. (2) Queen Elizabeth II Hospital, Howlands, Welwyn Garden City; tel. 07073 28111.

Kent: (1) Bethlem Royal Hospital, Monks Orchard Road, Beckenham; tel. 01–777 6611. (2) Bexley Hospital, Old Bexley Lane, Bexley; tel. 0322 526 282. (3) Kent & Canterbury Hospital, Ethelbert Road, Canterbury; tel. 0227 66877.
Leeds: Leeds Addiction Unit, 40 Clarendon Road, Leeds LS2 9PJ; tel. 0532 450970.
Leicester: Towers Hospital, Humberstone; tel. 0533 767 184.
Liverpool: Sefton General Hospital, Smithdown Road, Liverpool; tel. 051 733 4020.
London: (1) Charing Cross Hospital, 57 Aspenlea Road, W6; tel. 01–385 8834. (2) Hackney Hospital, Homerton High Street, E9; tel. 01 986 6816. (3) The London Hospital (St Clement's), 2a Bow Road, E3; tel. 01–980 4899 ext. 237 or 01–981 3266. (4) Maudsley Hospital, Denmark Hill, SE5; tel. 01–703 6333. (5) Queen Mary's Hospital, Roehampton Lane, SW15; tel. 01–789 6611 ext. 309. (6) St George's Hospital, Clare House, Blackshaw Road, SW17; tel. 01–672 1255 ext. 4098/99. (7) St Giles Hospital, St Giles Road, SE5; tel. 01–703 0898. (8) St Mary's Hospital, Woodfield Road, W9; tel. 01–286 7371/2. (9) St Thomas' Hospital, Lambeth Palace Road; SE1. tel. 01–633 0720. (10) Tooting Bec Hospital, Tooting Bec Road, SW17; tel. 01–672 9933. (11) University College Hospital, 122 Hampstead Road, NW1; tel. 01 387–9300 ext. 452/3/5. (12) Westminster Drug Treatment Unit, 52–53 Vincent Square, SW1; tel. 01–828 9811 ext. 397.
Manchester: Prestwich Hospital, Prestwich, Manchester; tel. 061 773 2236.
Merseyside: see Birkenhead, Chester, Liverpool under separate headings. (1) St Helen's Hospital, Marshalls Cross Road, St Helen's, Lancs; tel. 0744 26633. (2) Winwick Hospital, Winwick, Lancs; tel. 0925 55211.
Middlesborough: South Tees Health Authority Psychological Service, 22 Belle Vue Grove, Grove Hill, Middlesborough; tel. 0642 827 638.
Middlesex: (1) West Middlesex Hospital, Isleworth; tel. 01–560 2121. (2) St Bernard's Hospital, Southall; tel. 01–843 0736.
Newcastle-upon-Tyne: St Nicholas' Hospital, Gosforth; tel. 0632 850151.
Northampton: St Crispin's Hospital, Dunston, Northampton; tel. 0604 52323.

Norwich: West Norwich Hospital, The Yare Clinic, Bowthorpe Road; tel. 0603 28377.

Nottingham: Mapperley Hospital, Porchester Road, Nottingham; tel. 0602 608144.

Oxford: Littlemore Hospital, Oxford; tel. 0865 45651.

Portsmouth: St James' Hospital, Locksway Road, Portsmouth; tel. 0705 735211 ext. 294.

Rochdale: Birch Hill Hospital, Rochdale, Lancs; tel. 0706 77777.

Scarborough: St Mary's Hospital, Dean Road, Scarborough; tel. 0723 376111.

Sheffield: (1) Northern General Hospital, Herries Road; tel. 0742 382121. (2) Royal Hallamshire Hospital, Glossop Road; tel. 0742 26484.

Southampton: Royal South Hants Hospital, Fanshawe, Southampton; tel. 0703 34288.

Stafford: St George's Hospital, Milford Ward, Stafford; tel. 0785 3411 Ext 243.

Surrey: (1) Rees House Day Hospital, 214 Moreland Road, East Croydon; tel. 01–654 8100. (2) Brookwood Hospital, Knaphill, Surrey; tel. 04867 4545. (3) Henderson Hospital, 2 Homeland Drive, Sutton, Surrey; tel. 01–661 1611.

West Sussex: (1) Crawley Hospital, West Green Drive, Crawley; tel. 0293 27866. (2) Roffey Park Hospital, Horsham, West Sussex; tel. 0293 83561. (3) St Christopher's Day Hospital, Hurst Road, Horsham; tel. 0403 4367.

Wales

Cardiff (1) University Hospital of Wales, Heath Park, Cardiff; tel. 0222 755 944. (2) Whitchurch Hospital, Whitchurch, Cardiff; tel. 0222 62191.

Gwent: St Cadocs Hospital, Caerleon, Gwent; tel. 0633 421 121.

Powys: Llandrindod Wells Hospital, Hazels Clinic, Powys; tel. 0597 2951.

Northern Ireland

Shaftesbury Square Hospital, 116–118 Great Victoria Street, Belfast; tel. 0232 29808.

SERVICES IN SCOTLAND
This section includes NHS hospitals which offer services to
people with drug problems; community-based projects;
support groups for relatives and friends; and residential
facilities. Information supplied by SCODA's Scottish Office,
Glasgow.

NHS hospitals (patients seen by appointment)
Dumfries: Crichton Royal Hospital, Glencairn Unit; tel. 0387
55301. In-patient and out-patient facilities.
Dundee: Royal Dundee Liff Hospital, Liff by Dundee; tel.
0382 580 441. In-patient and out-patient facilities.
Edinburgh: Royal Edinburgh Hospital, Andrew Duncan
Clinic, Morningside Terrace; tel. 031 447 2011. Out-patients
only. GP- or self-referral. Facilities for detoxification and
individual counselling.
Glasgow area: (1) Duke Street Hospital, 5 Oakley Street,
Glasgow; tel. 041 554 6267. (2) Gartnavel General Hospital,
Ward 1A, 1053 Great Western Road, Glasgow; tel. 041 334
8122. (3) Leverndale Hospital, 510 Crookston Road, Glasgow;
tel. 041 882 6255. (4) Southern General Hospital, Drug
Stopping Clinic, Govan Road, Glasgow; tel. 041 445 2466 ext.
3300. Day project for problem drug-users. Hours: Monday–
Friday, 1.30 pm–5 pm. (5) Stobhill General Hospital,
Psychiatric Unit, Glasgow G21; tel. 041 558 0111. (6)
Woodilee Hospital, Lenzie; tel. 041 776 2451. Out-patient
clinic held at Denmark Street Health Centre, Possil.
Roxburghshire: Dingleton Hospital, Melrose; tel. 089 682
2506. In-patient and out-patient facilities.

Community-based projects (Glasgow area)
ALBAN HOUSE, 3 Cavendish Street, Glasgow G5; tel. 041
429 0237. Dry day centre for recovering alcoholics. Also
provides information, advice and support for drug-users and
their families. Assessment for referral to Residental Drug
Rehabilitation Project, St Peter's Seminary, Cardross.
CASTLEMILK DRUG MISUSE PROJECT, c/o Social
Work Department, 15 Dougrie Terrace, Castlemilk, Glasgow
G45; tel. 041 634 0331. Contact Colin Kirk at this address.

DENMARK STREET DAY PROJECT, Denmark Street
Health Centre, Possil, Glasgow G22; tel. 041 336 5311. Joint
Health Board/Social Work Department project providing
information, advice and counselling for drug-users and their
families.
DRUMCHAPEL ADDICTION ADVICE CENTRE, 234
Kinfauns Drive, Drumchapel, Glasgow G15; tel. 041 944
4242. Day centre. Counselling and advice for people with
alcohol or drug problems and their families. Information for
schools.
EASTERHOUSE CAMPAIGN ON DRUG ABUSE
(ECODA), 8–12 Arnisdale Road, Easterhouse, Glasgow G34;
tel. 041 773 2255. Information, advice and counselling for
drug-users and their families. Hours: Monday, Tuesday,
Wednesday, 1 pm–5 pm; Friday, 1 pm–4 pm.
POSSIL DRUG LINE, c/o Social Work Department, 42
Allander Street, Glasgow G22; tel. 041 336 3316. Confidential
advice and support for drug-users and their families by local
trained volunteers; immediate response when possible. Hours:
Monday and Tuesday, 12–4 pm.
THE PLACE, St Matthew's Rectory, 200 Balmore Road,
Possil, Glasgow G22; tel. 041 336 8147. Drop-in advice and
information centre for drug-users. Two beds for short-stay
detoxification.
ST ENOCH'S CENTRE, 13 South Portland Street, Glasgow
G5; tel. 041 429 5342. Day rehabilitation project for problem
drug-users. Hours: Monday–Friday, 10 am–4 pm.

Community-based projects (Strathclyde)
Ayr: (1) Area Unit (Addiction, rehabilitation and advice
service), Dalmilling Road, Ayr; tel. 0292 260122. (2) Out-
Reach worker for Ayr Angus Spankie, Ayr Social Work Area
Team, New Road, Ayr; tel. 0292 267675.
Irvine: Irvine Town Head Centre, 45 Town Head, Irvine; tel.
0294 75631. Project funded by Urban Aid; operates as an
addiction centre.
Kilmarnock: Out-Reach worker for Kilmarnock Alison Gracie
is based within Kilmarnock Social Work Area Team, 2 The
Cross, Kilmarnock; tel. 0563 28011 ext. 31.

Saltcoats: The Vernon Centre, 35 Vernon Street, Saltcoats;
tel. 0294 66325. An Urban Aid project which operates as an
addiction centre.

Support groups for relatives and friends (Glasgow)
FAMILIES ANONYMOUS, 8 Woodside Crescent, Glasgow
3; tel. 041 332 5463. Self-help group for relatives and friends
of problem drug-users. Medical advice available. Meetings:
Thursdays, 7.30 pm.
FAMILY SUPPORT GROUP, Duke Street Hospital, Duke
Street, Glasgow; tel. 041 556 5222 ext. 266. Support for
families. Meetings: Wednesdays 7 pm–8 pm.

Community-based projects (Edinburgh)
GATEWAY EXCHANGE, Abbey Mount, Regent Road,
Edinburgh; tel. 031 661 0982. Day centre offering information
and advice; individual and group therapy; counselling.
LEITH PROJECT, 36 Henderson Street, Leith, Edinburgh;
tel. 031 553 5250. Telephone advice and counselling service on
an appointment basis.
SHADA (Support, Help, Advice, Drug Abuse), c/o
Muirhouse Area Social Work Department, 34 Muirhouse
Crescent, Edinburgh; tel. 031 332 2314.
SIMPSON HOUSE, 52 Queen Street, Edinburgh; tel. 031
225 6028. Day centre which includes activities and group
sessions. DNA [Drug and Narcotics Anonymous] also holds
meetings at Simpson House.
WESTER HAILES 'HOTLINE', The Harbour, Wester
Hailes, Edinburgh; tel. 031 442 2465. Telephone advice
service. Emphasis on a Community Development approach,
working closely with community groups and Wester Hailes
Education Centre.

Residential facilities in Scotland (non-statutory)
Argyll: Ronachan House, Clachan, Tarbert, Argyll PA29
6XW; tel. 08804 252. Small number of problem drug-users
accepted on this residential project for alcoholics, which is run
by the Church of Scotland. Term: 6–12 months.
Dumbartonshire: St Peter's Seminary, Cardross,

Dumbartonshire; tel. 041 952 0996. Recently established residential project for problem drug-users. Referral through Alban House – see 'Community-based projects' for Glasgow.

SOME PRIVATE TREATMENT FACILITIES
Detoxification
HOLY CROSS HOSPITAL, Haslemere, Surrey; tel. 0428 3021. £660 for a week's stay.

Out-patient rehabilitation and counselling
SOUTHERN ADDICTION TREATMENT SERVICES, 47 High Street, Haslemere, Surrey; tel. 0428 3021. £25 per half-hour session. Services run by a physician. Limited number of assisted places for people who cannot afford full fee.
WESTERN COUNSELLING SERVICES, Weston-super-Mare; tel. 0934 415711.

Residential rehabilitation
BROADWAY LODGE, Old Mixon Road, Weston-super-Mare, Avon; tel. 0934 812319. This is a charity, a registered nursing home and treatment centre for chemical dependence, with 41 beds. Fees £95 per day inclusive, with vacancies at very short notice. A number of beds are available for those who cannot afford full fees, with waiting list of about three-and-a-half months.
BROADREACH HOUSE, 465 Tavistock Road, Plymouth, Devon; tel. 0752 774275.
CLOUDS HOUSE, East Knoyle, Wiltshire; tel. 074 783 650.
CHARTER CLINIC CHELSEA, 1 Radnor Walk, London SW3; tel. 01–351 1272.
CHARTER CLINIC HAMPSTEAD, 11 Fellowes Road, London NW3; tel. 01–586 8062.

REPUBLIC OF IRELAND
HEALTH EDUCATION BUREAU, 34 Upper Mount Street, Dublin 2; tel. Dublin 762393/761116/766640. This national organization has good illustrated educational and advice literature, available free through local Health Boards. It

may also be obtained by writing to or calling personally at the Bureau's office.

DRUGS ADVISORY AND TREATMENT CENTRE, Jervis Street Hospital, Dublin 1; tel. Dublin 748412/723355 ext. 366. This is the Republic's principal medical centre for the treatment of drug-abuse problems. In-patient and out-patient services.

BALLYMUN YOUTH ACTION PROJECT, 1A Balcurris Road, Ballymun, Dublin 11.

COOLMINE THERAPEUTIC COMMUNITY, Coolmine Lodge, Clonsilla, Co Dublin; tel. Dublin 214545/216564. Drug-free rehabilitation for 18–30-year-old people with drug or alcohol problems.

DONORE AVENUE YOUTH PROJECT, The Small Club, St Theresa's Gardens, Donore Avenue, Dublin 8; tel. Dublin 755420.

FAMILIES ANONYMOUS Hours: (1) Monday, 8 pm, Health Clinic, Patrick Street, Dun Laoire, Co Dublin; (2) Monday, 8 pm, St Theresa's Gardens, Donore Avenue, Dublin 8; (3) Wednesday, 8 pm, Community Centre, Mount Merrion, Dublin; (4) Friday, 8 pm, 1A Balcurris Road, Ballymun, Dublin 11.

MATER DEI INSTITUTE OF EDUCATION, Clonliffe Road, Dublin 3; tel. Dublin 376027. Counselling service for 11–18-year-olds by specialist psychologists.

NARCOTICS ANONYMOUS, PO Box 1368, Sheriff Street, Dublin 1.

RUTLAND CENTRE, Knocklyon House, Knocklyon Road, Templeogue, Dublin; tel. Dublin 946358/946972/946761. A drug-free therapeutic community for people with drug or alcohol problems.

TALBOT DAY CENTRE, 26 Upper Sherrard Street, Dublin 1 (moving to 29 Upper Buckingham Street, Dublin 1); tel. Dublin 747492.

TRANX RELEASE, PO Box 1378, Sheriff Street, Dublin 1.

Select bibliography

Baron, Dr Jason, *Kids and Drugs* (Perigee Books, New York, 1984).

Bestic, Alan, *Turn Me On Man* (Tandem, 1966).

Birdwood, Dr George, *The Willing Victim* (Secker & Warburg, 1969).

De Quincey, Thomas, *Confessions of an English Opium-Eater* (John Camden Hotten, 1877 edition, and Dent, 1960).

Edwards, G., and Busch, C. (ed.), *Drug Problems in Britain* (Academic Press, 1981).

Freemantle, Brian, *The Fix* (Michael Joseph, 1985).

Glatt, M.M. and Marks, J. (ed.), *The Dependence Phenomenon* (MTP Press, Lancaster, 1982).

Laurie, Peter, *Drugs* (Penguin, 1971 and 1978 editions).

Leech, Kenneth, *What Everyone Should Know About Drugs* (Sheldon Press, 1983).

McAlhone, Beryl, *WHERE on Drugs* (Advisory Centre for Education, 1971).

Meacher, Michael, *Cold Comfort* (House of Commons, 1985).

O'Donoghue, Noreen and Richardson, Sue (ed.), *Pure Murder* (Women's Community Press, Dublin, 1984).

Parish, Dr Peter, *Medicines: a guide for everybody* (Penguin, 1979, 1980 and 1982 editions).

Plant, M.A., *Drugs in Perspective* (Hodder and Stoughton, 1981).

Society of Civil and Public Servants (Customs and Excise Group), *Prevention and Control of Hard Drugs: Evidence for Home Affairs Committee* (1985), available from SCPS, 124 Southwark Street, London SE1; tel. 01–928 9671.

Willis, Dr James, *Drug Dependence* (Faber, 1969).

Willis, Dr James, *Addicts: Drugs and Alcohol Re-examined* (Pitman, 1974).

(Publishers are in London unless otherwise quoted.)

The pushers

It is close to midnight as a youth presses the doorbell of a flat on the twelfth floor of a high-rise block in a Merseyside town. He does not expect the door to open in response to the standard three-ring signal. When he pushes a £5 note through the letterbox, someone on the inside pushes out a small packet containing a minute quantity of heroin. He hurries away quickly, relieved to have 'scored', and to have beaten off the fear of heroin withdrawal for another few hours at least.

Down in the street, in a car parked a discreet distance away, a policeman keeps watch as clients come and go. He has seen it all before on countless occasions in this neighbourhood. But the police are not yet ready to move against the pusher on the twelfth floor, or against the dozen or so other dealers who operate in this council block and the surrounding area.

When officers of the Merseyside Drugs Squad were ready to call on some of these dealers, television cameras were present to record the events for BBC1's award-winning documentary programme *The Pushers* (9 January 1985). According to some local young people who were in a position to judge, the programme painted an authentic picture of an all-too-familiar situation, their only complaint being that you would not see the police being so polite in real life as they appeared on the programme.

The scenes shown were real enough, nevertheless. At the end of the film the pusher, George (not his real name), was seen being interviewed behind bars, at the start of a three-and-a-half year sentence. We learnt that he had a wife and a nine-month-old baby and that his brother was also in prison for heroin offences. Apart from missing his family and wishing he were not faced with a long spell in jail, he had few regrets, he told Paul Hamann, the programme's producer. When asked if he had ever worried about the consequences to his clients of his dealing in heroin he said, 'No, I was just thinking of myself – of my own habit.'

At the time of his arrest, George was using 1½ grams of heroin a day, at a cost of about £100. He did not deal in £5 bags or wraps, he told Detective Constable Brendon Farrell. Instead, he sold heroin in grams (at £65), half-grams (£35), and quarter-grams (£20). About every two days he bought in a quarter of an ounce of heroin, on which he could make a profit of about £90. (One ounce in apothecaries' measure equals 30 grams.) When analyzed, the heroin content of the brown powder found in his home was 30 per cent pure, which many would consider high. However, an analyst reckoned that heroin picked up on Merseyside tended to be about 42 per cent pure.

'Most people who smoke heroin have to sell it at some time in their lives, because that is the way it works,' explained Bill, another dealer. 'I've been doing it full-time for three or four years now. I first started buying ounces and selling half-ounces and quarter-ounces, but I went down on my luck – smoked too much heroin – and now it's just the grams. We buy a gram, divide it into fourteen or fifteen £5 wraps and what is left over we smoke ourselves. That's how we keep out habit going.'

There was no money to be made from pushing heroin if you were a smoker yourself, Bill continued. 'It's very rare for pushers to make money unless they go into it for the money. But usually, however much you sell, that is how much you smoke.' When asked what local people thought of drug-pushers, he replied, 'They don't like them. Quite a few have been beaten up or had their windows smashed. You always get a lot of abuse, and when they look at you it is as killers of their sons and daughters.'

'But aren't you killing their sons and daughters?' Paul Hamann asked.

'No, they are killing themselves,' Bill insisted. 'They're killing themselves the way we are. I know quite a few people who snatch handbags to get their money. I'd sooner sell heroin than go out mugging old ladies.'

Ken explained: 'I don't twist anyone's arm to buy it. I'm just trapped like everybody else. There isn't any one of them who wouldn't sell it, given the opportunity. You've got to do something. You either steal or you sell heroin, one of the two. I always feel guilty. Nobody does it by choice except the dealers who don't smoke it – the ones who are making all the money. I do it because if I didn't do this, I would be out robbing. I don't want to rob any more because I don't want to go back to prison again. But you've got to have it. I've woken up in the morning and I've started crying, because from the second you open your eyes it's like someone dropping a ton of bricks on you. All you can think about is where am I going to get the money? I've got to have it.'

There were others, however, for who dealing in heroin had promised to be a highly lucrative business. 'About two years ago I was doing really well,' Eric explained. 'I was selling about an ounce a day quite easily, and the profits worked out at around £4,000 or £5,000 a week. But I wasn't quite making that much because I was smoking something like four grams a day, and my wife was smoking too, costing about £300 a day. I was still managing to put away quite large amounts of money, and then it all dried up – you couldn't get any 'smack' anywhere for about two weeks.

'I had about £18,000 or £19,000 saved up at the time, and I just spent the lot because you couldn't get it [heroin] anywhere, and what little you could get was costing you the earth. I should have a beautiful home, but I sold everything out of it, absolutely everyhting. If it wasn't nailed down it got sold, because when I hit the bad patch I smoked all my profits away. I smoked all the gear away. I sold everything. You know it's a terrible waste but you just can't help yourself.'

The strain of living constantly in a state of siege, knowing that your home could be raided by the police at any moment, was described by another dealer: 'All you're thinking about is the door being burst open and the Drugs Squad coming in. Maybe your wife and kids are going to be there. Every time a car pulls up outside you jump up to look out the window. You're really scared stiff all the time. I've known people who've had a nervous breakdown just through the pressure involved. But you're caught in a trap. . .'

'Do you ever feel sorry for the pushers?' Brendon Farrell was asked.

'No, I don't feel sorry for the pushers. They live on other people's misery. They are just the lowest form of human life, in my estimation. I feel sorry for users, obviously. You wouldn't be human not to feel sorry for them, when you see the lifestyle they end up with, and the way they destroy their whole lives. Some pushers are in it solely to make money – they are referred to around here as "bread heads" – and they are the worst of all. They can see the misery they are causing and they just sit back laughing, riding around in their expensive cars. Then you have the other pusher, who is selling heroin basically to support his own habit, but he still keeps on selling once he has secured his own supply.'

For younger and less experienced people, the idea of earning big money for very little effort can be a powerful inducement, Detective Sergeant Keith Raybould explained. 'Put yourself in their position. These lads are getting something in the region of £20 a week benefit. If they can increase that ten-fold and make a couple of hundred pounds a day, then they're going to do it and there is nothing to stop them. We stop kids on the street who are literally teenagers, and invariably they will have £300, £500 or £1,000 in their possession. When you ask them what they are doing with that amount of cash, or where they got it, they will say they've won it on horses or it's savings. Obviously, we realize that they can't save that much money from their benefits, but it's very difficult to prove that the money has come from dealing in heroin.'

A young man being questioned was found to have £280 in his possession. He said that he had been saving up to buy a car, but nobody was convinced. 'This young man is seventeen years of age and he is unemployed,' Brendon Farrell explained. 'He's got £280 in his possession, and he has £10 worth of heroin – £10 worth of death – and that's what it's all about.'

No one was thinking in such terms at the stage when heroin was being introduced on Mereyside, he recalled. 'Suddenly, it seemed to be the "in" thing. The people who were selling it told everybody that you don't have to inject and so you don't become addicted, so they started smoking it. . . When you look at this piece of silver foil, the box of matches and the little bit of dust, it doesn't look very dangerous. On the other hand, if you look at a hypodermic syringe and needles, and a piece of rubber to wrap round your arm to bring the vein up, and you ask the average punter which one he wants, he's going to look at the silver foil and think that it can't do much harm.'

In an article in *The Listener* (10 January 1985) to coincide with the televising of *The Pushers*, Detective Constable Farrell recalled a particularly harrowing experience: 'One case that will live with me for the rest of my life began with a routine raid on a house in search of heroin. I knocked on the front door and was allowed in by the male occupant. It was approximately 12 noon. I could see from his demeanour that he was under the influence of some drug. We found his wife in bed, in a similar state. . . We started to search the premises. I chose one of the bedrooms which appeared not to be in use. I was confronted with a smell that cannot be described.

'The windows had been sealed with tape in a feeble effort to stop draughts. The room was so full of rubbish that it was near-impossible to search. I heard a noise coming from one corner. In a cot was a baby aged eight months. She was lying on her back, attempting to position the teat on a sauce bottle (which contained cold tea) into her mouth. I reached into the cot to pick her up and saw that her little arms appeared to have no strength in them, which made me think that they were broken. . . I immediately took the child to a local hospital and she was taken into care.'

He explains that when he joined the Drug Squad in the late

'seventies, cannabis was the main focus of police attention. 'There were only six people in the Wirral who were using opiates, which were usually the proceeds of burglaries at chemists' shops. Then the whole scene started to change. Searching houses for cannabis, I began finding pieces of silver foil with burn traces on them.'

Thus it was that the heroin problem which has now reached such alarming proportions crept in insidiously, taking the police in most parts of Britain by surprise. As the officers in a South London District Drugs Unit explain in chapter 6, it is only in the past year or so that extra resources have been made available in many areas to enable police to mount a realistic campaign against street dealers. Even now, their own unit would need three of four times the number of staff currently involved to tackle the local problem effectively.

Critics of official attitudes to the present drugs problem insist that the government's 1985 initiatives are too little and too late: all the pointers calling for prompt intervention were discernible to those working in the field as long ago as 1981, but their warnings went unheeded.

Where parents are aware that their children have been using heroin for four or five years, and are able to identify dealers, it is not surprising that they feel angry and impatient at what they judge to be tardiness on the part of the police in failing to make arrests.

'What people don't always realize it that there is no point in bringing a suspected pusher to court unless we have hard evidence, and it can take a long time to get this,' a senior policeman explained. 'We are in a situation in which there is collusion between dealer and clients, and both parties have a vested interested in keeping their business secret. Then when one pusher is picked up, a relative or friend in the same block or a nearby street takes over, and we have to begin all over again.'

In these circumstances, many parents sometimes feel the urge to go out and confront the people who are supplying their children. But even in neighbourhoods where the families of dealers and their clients are well known to each other, this seems to happen only very occasionally. 'It's better that way, because I couldn't trust myself alone with the monster who is selling heroin to my son,' said the father of a 16-year-old boy who had been using the drug for over two years.

One group of parents whose campaign led to a determined but non-violent confrontation with the dealers was the Dublin Concerned Parents Committee, whose successes attracted considerable publicity throughout 1984. The sudden eruption of a serious heroin problem among young adolescents appears to have many features in common

171

with a similar development in an area such as Merseyside. For instance, in 1981 heroin abuse was not a subject which came in for much discussion, but everyone seemed to be concerned about a steep rise in handbag snatches, muggings and burglaries attributed to a sudden increase in lawlessness among young people.

As late as 1982 there were official denials that Dublin had a drugs problem, but a survey carried out that year by Dr John Bradshaw on behalf of the Medico-Social Research Board showed that 12 per cent of those aged from fifteen to nineteen years were using heroin in the working-class areas of north-central Dublin. Even more surprising was the figure for girls, of whom 13 per cent were found to be heroin-users. The survey also found that the majority of heroin-users were injecting the drug, and that most were using other drugs in addition to heroin. It was suggested that Dublin's inner city had a drug problem comparable with that of some of the worst-affected ghettos of New York.

Some attempts to assess the size of the problem numerically have come up with as estimate of 1,500 heroin addicts and a further 3,000 occasional users in the city. About 1,000 people annually are treated for heroin addiction at the National Drugs Advice and Treatment Centre in Jervis Street, which has only nine in-patient beds and no residential facilities for people under sixteen years. The total figure is likely to be more than three times this number, it is claimed. Drug-related deaths were likely to be at least double the official figure, according to Jim Comberton, chairman of the Coolmine therapeutic centre. He was commenting on the death from heroin overdose of a 17-year-old youth who had been using drugs since the age of fourteen (*Irish Times*, 10 November 1984). Until that date, nine drug-related deaths had been recorded for the year.

At local level, in areas like St Theresa's Gardens – a complex of Dublin Corporation flats housing 400 families, with an unemployment rate of nearly 60 per cent among people of working age – the signs of serious drug abuse were inescapable. It was not uncommon for children to pick up discarded syringes and needles. 'The sight of addicts "fixing" in the stairwells was so common that people stepped over them casually,' Eamonn McCann, a Dublin journalist, reported in the *New Statesman* (18 May 1984). Flats were being used openly as distribution centres, but the police claimed it was almost impossible to find evidence which would stand up in court.

In Dublin the sale of heroin was soon found to be a particularly lucrative business. Supplies purchased in London at about £80 a gram could be sold in Dublin for up to four times that figure. There were

172

reports of the involvement of criminal 'godfathers' at the top end of the market and, indeed, some leading Dublin criminals have gone to prison for drug offences. At street level, children were being introduced to heroin by dealers who met them outside schools in working-class areas. 'In my area it was 10 packs of heroin for free,' revealed Tony Gregory, a Dublin teacher and politician, in an interview with *The Observer* (8 March 1984).

Now an independent member of the Irish Parliament, Tony Gregory had earned himself a reputation as a radical campaigner on welfare and housing issues long before heroin abuse emerged as a widespread problem in the inner city. He was the only MP to become involved in the Concerned Parents campaign, and in the *New Statesman* article he describes the atmosphere at the early parents' meetings, which began in June 1983, as 'electrifying'.

'I've never known anything like it before,' he recalled. 'There were scenes of great human drama, with mothers getting up in tears to say that they had put their sons out of the house because they wouldn't stop pushing. . . This was a great and genuine phenomenon, a community suddenly coming together out of revulsion at what was being done to them.'

Initially, Concerned Parents thought it would be possible to get the local authority to take action against known dealers who were living in Dublin Corporation housing. But they were told that it would take two years to obtain an eviction order. In *Pure Murder: a book about drug use* (edited by Noreen O'Donohue and Sue Richardson, Women's Community Press, Dublin, 1984), Willie Martin, a voluntary community worker at St Theresa's Gardens, explains how three local mothers asked him to arrange a meeting. There were women in each block who were trying to keep 'junkies' away from the stairways, but they admitted to having been intimidated by the sheer numbers – and verbal abuse – of the drug-users.

Once a sufficiently large number of parents was involved, they found that it was possible to gain control not only over the stairways, but also over access to their own respective blocks by non-resident drug-users. 'This plan worked very well. Parents stood on the corner and politely refused admission to outside junkies.' But it was soon realized that something more tangible needed to be done to curtail the supply of heroin.

At one meeting it was decided that a small delegation should be organized to visit known pushers and offer them a choice between stopping the sale of heroin in the flats and moving out altogether. All of those approached said they would stop selling heroin, but no one can place too much reliance on a dealer's word. Round-the-clock patrols were organized to prevent outsiders from coming in to buy heroin. These manoeuvres were making it more difficult for some pushers to do business, but their clients could still obtain supplies elsewhere.

One positive development was that the movement was growing rapidly in terms of numbers and morale. Within months the attendance at weekly meetings had risen to about 300, and despair was giving way to angry determination to 'drive the pushers out'. Eamonn McCann recalls the meeting which turned into a march, when hundreds of people chanting 'Pushers out!' closed in upon the homes of three dealers and evicted them. The dealers returned for their furniture and other belongings, but they made no attempt to regain possession of their flats.

This was the beginning of a process which was repeated frequently in other areas of the inner city during the following six months. 'A certain formality was introduced: suspected pushers were invited to attend crowded meetings in schools and community halls, confronted with evidence – statements from addicts and addicts' parents – and then told to get out of the drugs trade or out of the neighbourhood. The meetings were chaotic and emotional. Exchanges were unrestrained, and the justice being dispensed rough and ready. But it worked. The inexorable growth of the heroin problem had been reversed.'

What must seem an extraordinary aspect of this story is the low profile of the police during these activities, although, according to Eamonn McCann, they 'hovered in the background' while evictions were taking place. Another strange aspect is the absence of any reports in Dublin newspapers until after the pushers had been evicted. Then 'the dominant theme of the coverage . . . was that mob rule had broken out and that stern measures were called for. Suddenly, Concerned Victims were the criminals and the pushers were the victims.' One explanation suggested for the ambivalent attitude of police and press was that because poor areas like those involved had been forgotten by officialdom for so long, no one in authority knew how to react in the face of such startling events.

In *Pure Murder*, the editors sum up the government's response to this situation as a preoccupation with regaining control. 'It could not stand by while groups of people acted independently of official bodies. The Concerned Parents groups and others like them arose because they and their children, friends and neighbours were at the heart of the problem. They were met with a wall of hysterical condemnation. The state had to open up treatment centres, because otherwise local groups would eventually have opened up their own. The fact remains, however, that these groups achieved results where the authorities had failed.'

Dublin still has its heroin problem; but it is a problem which has been brought under considerably greater control than was the case two years ago in inner-city areas. And the fight to regain this level of control has had other beneficial effects, as Eamonn McCann explains. 'What the anti-drugs campaign has given to inner-city Dublin is a sense of achievement, and that is a heady thing to happen to people who have grown used to being pushed around and pushed out of sight. At the end of an exultant late-night street party in Dolphin House last October, held to declare the area drug-free, John McCann, chairman of the local group, stood on a table to shout: "Always remember that nobody did this for us – we did it ourselves!" '

Willie Martin concludes in his article in *Pure Murder*: 'The media still continues to try to undermine the Concerned Parents groups. The police still haven't gone all out against the pushers. The government still hasn't implemented the necessary drugs programme. What really matters, however, is that the communities are uniting. People are once more controlling their own lives. My community, St Theresa's Gardens, now has a drug centre, where addicts can go for the advice and counselling they so desperately need. Many of them are now ex-addicts, and are fully involved in a youth development programme. One of them is a member of my own family, who at one time I didn't think would live very long. Looking out of my window I can see children playing in the gardens, adults talking and joking, and I realize: Yes, we have won!'

The moral of this story is not that we should all go out – however well-meaning and dedicated to non-violent action – and take the law into our own hands. It is surely that desperate situations call for desperate remedies, and that there is nothing to be gained by standing by helplessly while one's world falls apart. Self-help means campaigning to gain attention, and shouting until somebody hears your cry, and never more so than when our children's lives and future well-being are threatened by something as pernicious as the drugs menace.

Index

176